OTHER BOOKS BY JOHN CANEMAKER

The Animated Raggedy Ann and Andy (1977)

Winsor McCay—His Life and Art (1987)

By John Canemaker and Robert E. Abrams:
Treasures of Disney Animation Art (1982)

FELIX

THE TWISTED TALE
OF THE WORLD'S
MOST FAMOUS CAT

JOHN CANEMAKER

PANTHEON BOOKS   NEW YORK

Grateful acknowledgment is made to the following for permission to reprint previously published material:

EMI Music Publishing: Excerpt from the song lyrics "Felix Kept On Walking" by Ed E. Bryant and Hubert W. David. Copyright 1923 and renewed 1951 by Lawrence Wright Music Ltd. All rights assigned to EMI Music Publishing Ltd. Rights for the U.S. and Canada controlled and administered by Colgems-EMI Music Inc. All rights reserved. International copyright secured. Used by permission.

Famous Music Publishing Companies: Excerpt from the song lyrics "Felix the Wonderful Cat," words and music by Winston Sharples. Copyright © 1958 and 1961 by Felix The Cat Productions, Inc. Sole Selling Agent Famous Music Corporation. Reprinted by permission.

Sam Fox Publishing Company, Inc.: Excerpt from the song lyrics "Felix the Cat." Words by Alfred Bryan. Music by Pete Wendling and Max Kortlander. Copyright 1928 by Sam Fox Publishing Company, Inc. N.Y., N.Y. Used by permission.

Library of Congress Cataloging-in-Publication Data

Canemaker, John.
    Felix : the twisted tale of the world's most famous cat / John Canemaker.
        p.   cm.
    Includes bibliographical references.
    ISBN 0-679-40127-x
    1. Messmer, Otto—Criticism and interpretation.
2. Felix the Cat (fictitious character) 3. Animated films—
United States—History and criticism.   I. Title.
NC1766.U52M4734   1991
741.5′8′092—dc20   90-44245

Book Design by Peter A. Andersen
Manufactured in the United States of America
First Edition

For Sister Dymphna Leonard, R.S.H.M.,
gifted educator and friend

CONTENTS

Opposite: Britain first published a Felix the Cat comic strip in 1923. This example is from the periodical *Modern Boy*, February 1, 1936. Courtesy of David R. Williams.

Felix animation sketches,
c. 1924. Collection of Mark
Newgarden.

ACKNOWLEDGMENTS

THE COOPERATION and generosity of many individuals made re-searching the history of Felix the Cat a joy. My gratitude begins with the late Otto Messmer, who, in the 1970s, granted me several interviews (including one on camera for a film documentary) and provided a number of documents that served me well on the current project. Otto, his late wife, Anne, and their daughters, Doris and Jeanne, always made me feel welcome in their home. I am particularly indebted to Doris Messmer for making additional documents available to me since Otto's death in 1983.

I am grateful to the late Joe Oriolo, who discussed with me his significant role in Felix's story on a number of occasions and allowed me to photograph Pat Sullivan's 1924–1925 scrapbooks, which yielded valuable information.

Hal Walker and Al Eugster, the two surviving animators from Felix's heyday in the 1920s, responded to my numerous questions with patience and candid replies.

Milton and Irma Krents and Alfred and Gertrude K. Wasserstrom, members of the family of Harry Kopp (Pat Sullivan's lawyer), kindly provided remembrances, as well as artwork, photos, and letters. Robert and Katherine Fish, son-in-law and daughter of Margaret Winkler Mintz, generously arranged for me to meet the legendary Mrs. Mintz and to photograph her scrapbooks.

A special thank-you to my colleagues in the study of the history of animation and comics—J. Michael Barrier, Louise Beaudet of La Cinémathèque Québecoise, Jerry Beck, Howard Beckerman, Leslie

The "flipbook" that appears in the lower righthand corner of these pages consists of twenty-eight sequential drawings of Felix walking while thinking, animated by Otto Messmer for a 1955 Disneyland television program. Collection Walt Disney Archives.

Carbaga, Karl Cohen, Donald Crafton, Jerry Guldin of UCLA Film Archives, Mark and Cole Johnson, Pierre Lambert, Bill Lorenzo, Leonard Maltin, William Moritz, Mark Newgarden, Ronald Schwarz, Charles Solomon, Steve Schneider, David Watson, Cinémathèque Project Officer of the Museum of Contemporary Art, Sydney, Vane Lindesay, Robin Allan, David R. Williams, David R. Smith of Walt Disney Archives, Charles Silver and Ron Magliozzi of the Museum of Modern Art Film Study Center—for their extraordinary generosity in providing me with essential information, stills, artwork, and documents.

Bruce Abrams, New York City Chief Clerk Office Archivist, Evelyn Gonzalez and Kenneth Cobb, Research Archivists, and Idilio Gracia Peña, Director, of the Municipal Archives of the City of New York, and Murray Butchen, Assistant Deputy Chief Clerk, New York Supreme Court, facilitated my search through legal-system labyrinths, as they enthusiastically guided me to a treasure trove of dusty but information-filled contracts and court records.

I am grateful to Mike and Jeanne Glad, Felix Cappadona, Michael Del Castello, Keith Kaonis of *The Inside Collector* magazine, Philip and Cliff Samuels of Samuels Museum of Comic Toys, David Shepard, and Mark Newgarden for kindly providing photographs of their personal collections of Felix art, toys, and collectibles, and to Robert Del Tredici for making available his photographic portraits of Otto Messmer.

The following individuals generously granted interviews, volunteered special information and materials, or provided other assistances during the course of my research:

Marty Grebler of Ad-Link, Inc., Eric Alberta and Joshua Arfer of Christie's East, Roberta Y. Arminio, Blaine Bartell, Dora Bashour, Mel and Eunice Birnkrant, Mrs. Betty Buckley, Elaine Burrows of the British Film Institute, John Cocchi, Rich Conaty, Jack Damlos, Nancyann Dziedzic, Gary English, Milton Friedman, Martin Fox, Ira Gallen, Karen Gaughan, Graham Halky, Thomas W. Hoffer, Shirley Humphries, Deputy Mitchell Librarian at the State Library of New South Wales, Rudy Ising, Ollie Johnston, Chuck Jones, Phil Kimmelman, Richard Kluga, Richard Koszarski, Robert Lesser, Bob Links and Gene Phalen of Vidachrome, Harry Love, Mrs. John Lynch,

Donald W. Maloney, Arthur and Robert Markewich, Jerry Matthews, Henry Mazzeo, Jr., Joyce Moser, Glenn Myrent, Elaine Pichaske, Jon Quint, Betty Robertson, Maurice Sendak, Bernard Shine of The Shine Gallery, Dorothy Silva, Donald Spoto, Carol Stevens, Curtice Taylor, Frank Thomas, Edwin Walker, Glenn White, and George Winkler.

Joseph F. D'Angelo, Jeff Brown, and Ita Golzman of King Features Syndicate granted the necessary permissions to publish images of Felix in all his manifestations.

Robert Cornfield, my supportive literary agent, provided excellent advice during difficult times.

Martha Kaplan is one of the finest editors I have had the good fortune to work with. She encouraged me to take on this project, and she guided the book's progress with intelligence, sensitivity, and a marvelous sense of humor.

This is my fourth book, and once again the intelligent suggestions, advice, and companionship of Joseph Kennedy have sustained me.

This book is dedicated to Sister Dymphna Leonard, R.S.H.M., of Marymount Manhattan College, who changed the direction of my life in 1973 when she arranged my first interviews with animation pioneers and commissioned my first writings about animation history.

FELIX

INTRODUCTION

IN THE FALL of 1928, one year after the Warner brothers revolutionized movies with *The Jazz Singer*, the film industry was in chaos. The public's demand for "talkies" seemed insatiable, yet producers facing the technological obstacles and confusion of converting to sound feared making decisions of major financial consequence.

Equipment was scarce and expensive, studios had to build new soundproof stages, and to enter the international market, films would now have to be dubbed into foreign languages. Directors chafed at the loss of the camera's mobility that the new microphones brought, and stars deemed vocally inadequate saw their careers strangled by microphone wire.

The only certainty was that cinema's silent era was over. Producers and performers slow to adapt to the new technology, or worse, who chose to ignore it, did so at their peril. The same held true as much for the animated film as for live-action.

The Pat Sullivan studio was the most successful animation studio of the silent era and, by 1928, the most dangerously complacent. Sullivan's, at 47 West Sixty-third Street in New York City, was home to the world's greatest cartoon star, then at the zenith of his popularity: Felix the Cat.

For movie audiences around the world, Felix the Cat was as real, beloved, and recognizable as Charlie Chaplin and Buster Keaton. After almost a decade, the cinema cat's feisty screen personality, eloquent pantomime and facial expressions, his individualistic mannerisms (such

Opposite: Otto Messmer (left) and Pat Sullivan, about 1926. Collection La Cinémathèque Québecoise.

as pacing hands-behind-back while thinking), and his ability to solve problems in fantastic ways—often making imaginative use of his own body parts—were anticipated by moviegoers with joy.

People wanted to take cute, round Felix home with them and did, for his black-and-white image adorned over two hundred items of merchandise, including dolls, toys, books, clothing, and sporting goods. Felix was an animated icon of the optimistic, devil-may-care Roaring Twenties. Newspapers and magazines constantly "interviewed" him and photo spreads showed him dancing the Charleston and Black Bottom with pretty human starlets. Aviatrix Ruth Elder carried a stuffed Felix doll on her attempted transatlantic flight.

Felix's popularity cut through class, age, and cultural barriers. In 1927, over 15,000 midwestern children entered a Felix the Cat drawing contest, and the Felix comic strip, begun in 1923, appeared in more than sixty newspapers throughout the world. Wildly popular in England, Felix was made mascot for Britain's polo team by the Prince of Wales, and Queen Mary brought a model of the film cat home to King George.

Three Felix dolls, c. 1925, manufactured by Schoenhut. Collection Samuels Museum of Comic Toys.

Pop songs were written about him ("Felix Kept on Walking" in Britain and "Felix the Cat" in America), and Paul Hindemith, an avid fan, composed a score called *Felix at the Circus*. British caricaturist David Low said Felix advanced the art of animation "a couple of miles or so," a member of the Académie Française admired the "extraordinary personality" of Felix, and a German film theorist pondered Felix's "amazing world." George Bernard Shaw ruefully noted that if Michelangelo "were now alive I have not the slightest doubt that he would have his letter-box filled with proposals from the great film firms to concentrate his powers to the delineation of Felix the Cat instead of decorating the Sistine Chapel."

Felix the Cat's rise to stardom resulted from a symbiotic professional relationship between a shy artist and an aggressive entrepreneur. Otto Messmer, an unusually meek but highly creative cartoonist, devised and directed the films, and gave Felix his individuality—he was the first animated character in a film series to have a unique personality. Producer–studio owner Pat Sullivan was an unexceptional cartoonist but a good salesman, who fought for international distribution of the films and high-visibility merchandising contracts. It was a fortuitous combination, for Felix would not have gone as far as he did without the contributions of both men.

But the Sullivan-Messmer "partnership" was also grossly inequitable: Messmer never received public credit for his contributions to the Felix films nor did he own any rights in the character's lucrative image. All credit and moneys went to Sullivan, whose parsimony extended to the production of the films. They were made as cheaply as possible by limiting the size of the staff (and their salaries) and skimping on technology.

Sound, for example, was something Felix could do without, thought Sullivan, whose judgment was often dulled by alcohol, a lifetime addiction that would prove fatal professionally as well as personally.

"Why change?" he said, refusing to tamper with a magic formula that had, after a checkered life, finally brought him fame and fortune. He got no argument, as usual, from the passive Messmer, who years later recalled, "Felix was goin' so good, it seemed like he would go on forever."

Felix Cat (*sic*), mascot of Fighter Squadron 31, the "Tomcatters," an insignia emblazoned on the side of combat aircraft.

Ten blocks down Broadway from the Sullivan studio was the Colony Theatre, where on November 18, 1928, a lean and hungry seat-of-the-pants Hollywood producer of limited success stood at the back of the house listening to the audience's laughter. Twenty-six-year-old Walt Disney had gambled everything he owned on the film flickering on the screen: *Steamboat Willie*, the first animated cartoon with an imaginatively integrated sound track consisting of music, voices, and effects.

In the film, a character new to the public—a mouse named Mickey—made music from an astonishing assortment of "instruments," including a cat's tail, a cow's teeth, a goose's neck, and a pig's teats. To Disney's relief, audiences and critics roared their approval. The *New York Times* called Disney's film "an ingenious piece of work." The reviewer for *Exhibitor's Herald* found it "impossible to describe this riot of mirth, but it knocked me out of my seat." *Variety* raved, "It's a peach of a synchronization job all the way, bright, snappy and fitting the situation perfectly. . . . With most of the animated cartoons qualifying as a pain in the neck, it's a signal tribute to this particular one. . . ."

A few experimental sound cartoons had been produced before Disney came on the scene, but his innovative use of the technology made *Steamboat Willie* the *Jazz Singer* of animation. Like Al Jolson's hammy baritone, Mickey Mouse's squeak was a clarion call announcing profound changes in the movie industry.

Sullivan and Messmer heeded the call too late. Within two years,

the Mouse devoured the Cat. "Disney put us out of business with his sound," said a Felix animator, Hal Walker.

Following the demise of the Sullivan studio, Felix kept on walking, in the words of one of his theme songs. He held on in comic books and (until 1967) in a newspaper comic strip. In 1959, he began a new career on television.

Felix's comeback TV series ended years ago, and his vintage films of the twenties are rarely screened outside of academic or museum settings. Most moviegoers today have never seen Felix the Cat in action on a screen.

Yet, over seventy years after his creation, Felix is extremely popular. His face and shape—as easily recognizable as Mickey Mouse's—are embraced by the public on a variety of merchandise, such as dolls, toys, greeting cards, coffee mugs, watches, and numerous other products. In his early films, Felix was a triumph of personality, which was expressed in the way he moved. As a licensed image, Felix is not kinetic, yet his power to communicate remains undiminished.

Part of Felix's appeal may be our continuing fascination with cats, be they Bastet, the Cheshire, Krazy, or Garfield. But a major element of Felix's enduring magic is found in his simple, direct design, simultaneously primitive and modern, like a Lascaux bison.

Felix is a radical abstraction of "cat," as Mickey is a symbolic distillation of "mouse." Both characters exhibit a childlike cranial bulge

Sequential film frames from *One Good Turn* (1929). Collection of Mike and Jeanne Glad.

with big round eyes atop a small body, an image which triggers people's innate feelings of affection for babies. The construction of both Felix and Mickey is based on interlocking circles, a shape that subconsciously connects with sensual, pleasurable imagery. In addition, the circle symbolizes infinity and eternity; it denotes wholeness and continuity—survival. There is a feeling of reassurance about it. Felix's formula design is arguably more interesting than Mickey's; his pointed ears and whiskers lend variety to the basic circular form—the excitement of the unexpected, a hint of real feline sharpness and softness—in contrast to the blander all-circular mouse. ⌐

A rough drawing of Felix by Otto Messmer reveals the interlocking circular design of the character. Courtesy Doris Messmer.

Felix's survival is a tribute to his durability as a quintessential cartoon image. For from his debut in 1919 in a short called *Feline Follies*, through his comeback on television, Felix the Cat's career was underscored by human folly on a grand scale.

Opposite: A poster drawn by animator Dana Parker for *Felix the Cat Trips Through Toyland* (1925). Collection of Mark Newgarden.

Universal Film Manufacturing Company

TELEPHONE BRYANT 4434   CABLE ADDRESS·UNFILMAN

...LDING, BROADWAY AT...

NEW YORK   Dec. 21, 1915.

ANIMATED WEEKLY DEPARTMENT

TEL. BRYANT 1443   573 ELEVENTH AVENUE

AGREEMENT made this twenty-first day of December, 1915, by and between the Universal Film Mfg. Company, party of the first part, and Otto Messmer, party of the second part.

FIRST: Otto Messmer does hereby agree to make for the Universal Film Mfg. Company, a motion picture which shall be satisfactory to it and meet with its approval in every respect. In the event that said motion picture made by Otto Messmer as hereinabove provided, is satisfactory to and meets with the approval of the Universal Film Mfg. Company in every respect, then the Universal Film Mfg. Company shall pay to the said Otto Messmer the sum of Fifty ($50) Dollars.

IN THE EVENT that the motion picture made by the said Otto Messmer fails to meet with the approval of the Universal Film Mfg. Company, then the said Universal Film Mfg. Company shall turn over to the said Otto Messmer the negative and one (1) positive print of said motion picture.

NOTHING HEREIN CONTAINED shall be construed as requiring the Universal Film Mfg. Company to pay any sum or sums whatsoever to the said Otto Messmer, in the event that the motion picture made by him fails of its approval or is not satisfactory to the Universal Film Mfg. Company.

IN WITNESS HEREWITH the party of the second part has hereunto set his hand and seal, and the party of the first part has caused its presents to be signed in its name by its duly authorized officer.

Universal Film Mfg. Company.

Witnesses

Cecile Kauffman   Otto Messmer

Hollywood on the Hudson

BEFORE HOLLYWOOD'S sunny climate proved irresistible to moviemakers, the shooting locale of choice was northern New Jersey. In the days when Manhattan was the world's film capital, picturesque rural settings were a ferry ride away across the Hudson River. A quick trolley up the Palisades led to Fort Lee, an area so versatile in representing a variety of settings—from the Old West to the Old South—that in 1909 the first of several studios and film laboratories was built there.

By 1915, over a dozen studios were busy at work around the clock. The World Film Corporation studios, for example, run by Lewis J. Selznick, filmed one feature a week for five years, and usually half a dozen pictures were being shot simultaneously on the main stage.

For about a decade, life seemed to be one big costume party for local residents of Fort Lee. Cowboys clad in buckskin strode down Main Street with feather-bedecked Indians. Neighbors dressed in the gray and blue uniforms of Civil War soldiers walked alongside bewigged and ballgowned prerevolutionary "French aristocrats." The good citizens of Fort Lee were paid seven to twelve dollars a day for the privilege of dressing up and hobnobbing with movie stars by appearing as extras in the many films shot there.

One day they might be "background" in a D. W. Griffith Biograph film starring Mary Pickford, Lionel Barrymore, or Henry Walthall. The next day, extras might be needed at the Triangle Company for a wild Mack Sennett–directed comedy with Fatty Arbuckle and Mabel Normand.

Opposite: Otto Messmer's first movie contract, dated December 21, 1915. Courtesy Doris Messmer.

Otto Messmer (left) with his brother John, in 1894. Courtesy Doris Messmer.

Jobs were plentiful for people behind the cameras as well; carpenters, prop builders, and set painters were always in demand. Interiors were often painted on flats and shot on glass-enclosed stages that relied on the sun for illumination. The Paragon studio, located in a hollow on John Street, was considered the most modern studio of its day because of its banks of extremely hot and bright Cooper-Hewitt mercury lamps for night shooting.

On a hill above the Paragon was the Universal Film Manufacturing Company studio, owned by Carl Laemmle. One day in 1915, a twenty-three-year-old cartoonist named Otto Messmer came to the studio looking to "get into scene painting."

Messmer was a local, born on August 16, 1892, five miles south of Fort Lee in West Hoboken, an enclave of German immigrants now known as Union City. His father, John, "a crackerjack machinist," came from Bavaria and worked in the West Hoboken ironworks and silk mills. His mother, the former Theckla Kiesewetter, an American whose stepfather served in the Civil War, also worked in the silk mills.

Messmer's description of his father—"very gentle, efficient"—is the same way animators would later describe him. "We were all very quiet," Messmer recalled, except his outgoing brother, John, his elder by two years. The close-knit Roman Catholic family was a happy one, though "on the verge of being poor," said Messmer. "Steadily working, struggling along. But in those days, you didn't need much."

At Holy Family, a "strict" parochial school in West Hoboken, a Sister Rita helped Otto with spelling and drawing. "In this school," he said, "they had special drawing classes. And they had an awful lot of exhibitions for the public to come in and look at these little drawings."

After graduating from Holy Family School in 1907, Messmer was unsure of where his future lay, so he took an art correspondence course. ("They were very good in those days. You had to toe the mark.") He also attended evening classes for a number of years at the Thomas School of Art on Twenty-third Street in New York, where "they taught you to draw more 'straight,'" as opposed to cartoon-y. "They forced you to study fashion drawing for catalogues, women's gowns, so forth. They could get you a job while you continued your studies." The Thomas School found him part-time employment with the Acme

Agency illustrating fashion catalogues. "But I didn't like that," said Messmer. "I kept thinking about cartoons."

The theater also intrigued Otto. His mother and aunt would often take him to the Lyric in Hoboken to see vaudeville shows, road company dramas, and musicals, "every week a different one." Messmer painted stage scenery in 1912 for the Holy Family Dramatic Circle— shows with titles like *Miss Dolly Dollars* and *Red Pepper Minstrels*, and the Union City Passion Play. He was toying vaguely with the idea of becoming "a scenic painter, cause there were a lot of theaters. Movies were regarded as a little novelty." But movies also fascinated him, and he regularly visited the nickelodeons, at literally a nickel a show: "A man would rent an empty store with a lot of camp chairs and have a little screen. Then get a couple of [short film] reels and that was called the movies."

Otto's brother took him to see his first animated film in Winsor McCay's vaudeville act in New York. In 1911, the great newspaper cartoonist showcased his experiments with animation at the Colonial

Winsor McCay, the great comic-strip cartoonist and animator, and a drawing from his 1914 film masterpiece, *Gertie the Dinosaur*. Collection of the author.

Theatre on Manhattan's Upper West Side. He presented *Little Nemo*, derived from his world-famous comic strip, *Little Nemo in Slumberland*, and Messmer remembered it was "quite a thing to see drawings move." In 1912, he saw McCay's second film, *How a Mosquito Operates*. In early 1914, Messmer attended Hammerstein's Theatre on Forty-second Street to witness McCay's third film, a masterpiece of early personality animation, titled *Gertie the Dinosaur*. The performance was impressive not only because of the lifelike quality of the animation of the girlish diplodocus; it was also memorable because McCay appeared on stage in front of the movie screen and gave instructions to his "trained" cartoon dinosaur while cracking a bullwhip.

Messmer also saw some episodes of *The Newlyweds*, a series of thirteen cartoon films released between March 1913 and January 1914, based on George McManus's newspaper strip. The series was animated anonymously by France's Emile Cohl at the Eclair studio in Fort Lee and was an important influence in further associating animation with comics in the mind of the public and journalist cartoonists.

At home, Messmer began contributing gag cartoons to magazines and newspapers, and, always the polite Catholic boy, sent an inquiry to the editors first, asking if they were interested. *Fun*, the Sunday comics supplement of the *New York World*, paid Messmer eighteen to twenty dollars for each cartoon published.

A cartoon by Otto Messmer, published in the June 28, 1914, Sunday color supplement *Fun* in the *New York World* newspaper. Courtesy Doris Messmer.

Young Messmer's *Fun* cartoons display a witty pen line, an eye for motion and the telling detail, and considerable skill in the composition of figures in a limited space. The humor of most of the spot cartoons is based upon unexpected visual interpretations of familiar sayings: on June 21, 1914, for example, Messmer drew a formally dressed couple happily waltzing, a whirling visual counterpoint to the staid caption: "Extract from the minutes. 'All were in favor of the motion.' " The next week, Messmer drew young boys hiding baseball gloves and a bat and walking gingerly away from a distressed gent with a blackened eye and a baseball at his feet; the caption reads: "Baseball Terms. 'Game called on account of darkness.' "

Messmer usually signed his work with his full name or "O. Messmer"; but predicting the excessive humility which would lead in the near future to his receiving no public credit for Felix the Cat's success,

EXTRACT FROM THE MINUTES.
"All were in favor of the motion."

BASEBALL TERMS.
"Game called on account of darkness."

Messmer "got a little self-conscious having my name on them. Didn't think I was worth it. So I used a nom de plume once in a while: 'Otz.' That's what my nickname was."

Around this time, Messmer was also composing and selling humorous poems. One surviving published example demonstrates his verbal wit and agile talent for wordplay:

Two Messmer gag cartoons published in *Fun*: (left) June 21, 1914, and (right) June 28, 1914. Courtesy Doris Messmer.

Ode to an Old Straw Hat

Last spring when the winds grew warmer
I purchased me a lid.
Two bucks was the sum invested,
My winter hat I hid.

Of straw was the thing I purchased,
It cooled my shining pate,
But now, are my tear-drops falling
For part we must, 'tis fate.

'Tis weak, that I thus am sobbing
And I fain would'st can the weep,
But I sigh when I think of winter
When my straw lid must sleep.

Messmer's sales of cartoons and poems gave him "great encouragement." He happily quit his job at Acme, which, in any case, was "very seasonal. You only worked three months a year." Still intrigued with the theater and movies, and aware of the increase in film production in nearby Fort Lee, Messmer wrote twenty polite letters to as many studios requesting an interview as a set painter. "I got a nice letter from Universal," he said. So, armed with samples of his published cartoons, he took a trolley to Fort Lee to meet with Jack Cohn, who was "in charge of the newsreel."

"All I had to show was these comics I had sold," recalled Messmer. Among his samples was an animation experiment, probably a flipbook, reflecting the muted fear prevalent in America at the time regarding the war that had begun the year before in Europe. "There was a horrible feeling," he said. "The world had been very peaceful since the Civil War and the Spanish War. But there were rumblings of this European war. Preparedness was the word. We were so unprepared, we had no army at all. Our artillery was very old-fashioned.

"So in that spirit, it was only a kid's idea, I had an egg and a hen looked at a sign 'Preparedness—Wake Up, America! Are you prepared for war?' was the slogan. He [sic] was inspired now, you know? When the egg hatched there was some military tanks and stuff like that in there instead of a little chicken. Mr. Cohn liked it very well."

Cohn, who had been with Laemmle and Universal since 1908 and would later found Columbia Pictures with his brother Harry, was thinking of adding animated shorts to the weekly live-action Universal newsreel. Cohn was responding to the growing popularity of animated cartoons. Winsor McCay and Emile Cohl paved the way, but by 1915, new studios with many workers standardized the technology and, using assembly-line methods, were able to push out *series* of cartoons to eager moviegoers. Messmer's samples showed an obvious talent for humorous, inventive cartooning, and a rudimentary knowledge of animation, so Cohn signed the young man to a contract to make a test film. The agreement, dated December 21, 1915, makes no mention of animation or requirements for the content of the film; it simply agrees to pay Messmer fifty dollars if he makes "a motion picture which shall be satisfactory and meet [Universal's] approval in every respect."

A frame from *Le Cauchemar du Fantoche* (1908), a short film by Emile Cohl.

At home, Messmer dove into the assignment, even though he "didn't know how [he] would make it." That is, his animation technique was self-taught, with a few pointers picked up listening to Winsor McCay describe animation in his vaudeville act. Messmer knew that, according to McCay, each drawing had to be completely redrawn many, many times, backgrounds as well as the actual characters, to create the sensation of movement.

Messmer did not yet know of a laborsaving method, patented by John Randolph Bray in 1914, that revolutionized animation by turning it into an industry: the creation of "cels," clear sheets of celluloid acetate, on which sequential drawings of the characters are outlined in ink and painted, and photographed over an opaque background that need be drawn only once.

Nor did Messmer know of an earlier innovation—the peg system— for easily registering drawings one on top of the other, devised by Raoul Barre in 1913: two wooden pegs on top of the drawing board that match punched peg-holes on sheets of paper.

Messmer's father built him an animation drawing board with a light bulb shining underneath a pane of glass to enable him to see through several sheets of paper. Otto, however, used a "nice stiff cardboard" rather than a medium bond for his drawings, which must have been difficult to see through even with underlighting. As for registering the drawings, his father built a corner at the top of the board where Otto "fitted them in." Despite the difficulties, Messmer "moved 'em. One after the other."

The test animation starred a character Messmer named "Motor Mat," a fearless automobilist. "In those days," he said, "the roads were filled with horse-and-wagons. Very few automobiles. Motor Mat had a little car called a flivver. His horse didn't like it very much. The difficulties he had with that car was a lot of laughs. West New York was all goat fields, everybody had a goat. They pulled the carts for the kids. They used to chew on tin cans like chewing gum. So I had a goat bite one of the tires on Mat's flivver. It didn't bother [Mat]. He just takes his cigar out and blows a smoke ring and uses *that* for the tire. All picture gags. No matter what difficulty, he overcame it."

Messmer's first film already contained the personal stylistic motifs that would reoccur throughout his animation career and are best show-cased in the Felix the Cat series: the coolly detached yet determined protagonist, who uses his brain and the magic of metamorphosis to solve problems; the simple, direct pantomimic acting; dry wit expressed through visual puns.

Messmer took his Motor Mat drawings to Universal for photograph-ing. "They didn't have a special [animation] camera," he explained. "They used a table with big studio lights and a cameraman turning [the crank of the vertically mounted camera]." The cameraman, per-haps annoyed by Messmer's crude "corner" registration of the draw-ings, mentioned another animator who "comes in here, and hooks [the drawings over pegs]." (Unknown to Messmer at the time, this animator was Pat Sullivan. Universal rented their studio equipment to anyone for a small service fee.) For Messmer, the casually shared information completed his hit-and-miss knowledge about the mysterious animation processes. "I knew the whole thing instantly then," he said.

The drawings were shot on a live-action stage, amid a swirl of activity and noise from directors and actors shooting simultaneous photoplays. Messmer remembered "a big lion in a cage. They'd purposely get him hungry so he'd emote for the movies. Through the bars they'd pho-tograph him leaping." Despite roaring lions and shouting directors and actors, the methodical, tedious frame-by-frame shooting of Messmer's drawings attracted its share of attention. Slowly, "all those actors came around watching this new thing."

Motor Mat, according to Messmer, "turned out good, but they never released it." It led, however, to more work for the fledgling animator when Jack Cohn showed Messmer's animation drawings to two car-toonists who used Universal's facilities, Pat Sullivan and Henry "Hy" Mayer.

Hy Mayer was an internationally renowned cartoonist for a number of popular humor magazines and newspapers. For nearly two decades, he also produced film shorts in which he rapidly drew caricatures and humorous topical situations. (His seven-year association with the Uni-versal Weekly newsreel started in 1913.) He was an excellent drafts-man but not an animator.

Pat Sullivan was a former assistant to comic-strip cartoonist William

Otto Messmer, about 1914.
Courtesy Doris Messmer.

Opposite: Otto Messmer designed this 1923 poster. Collection of Mike and Jeanne Glad.

18

COMIC SUPPLEMENT
REGULAR FEATURE
EVERY DAY

BOSTON AMERICAN
The Largest Evening Circulation in New England

YOUR SUNDAY TREAT
EVERY DAY
IN THE WEEK

October 26, 1923

Felix

PAT SULLIVAN

A Felix comic book (March 1954, vol. 1, no. 51) with drawings by both Otto Messmer (the cover and the page on left) and Joe Oriolo.

Opposite: A comic strip dated October 26, 1923, two months after Felix made his debut in newspapers across the country. Collection of Mark Johnson.

Felix goes Fishing

Pascall

SMOKER'S
COMPANION SETS.

Prices ranging from
6d. *to* 7s. 6d.

Felix the Film Cat which appears
exclusively in Pathe's Eve and
Everybody's Film Review.

25
BARRATT & Cº.

Manufacturing
Confectioners.
Wood Green, LONDON.

FELIX
PICTURES.

a Series of
32
when joined
together form
a complete
Cinema.

Printed in Bavaria

"I met a few old friends at
Wembley!"

"Please Lord, excuse me while
I kick Felix!"

By the late 1920s Felix was advertising everything from British cigarettes (four cards above, courtesy David R. Williams) to pencils (courtesy Doris Messmer). He also appeared on British postcards (above right).

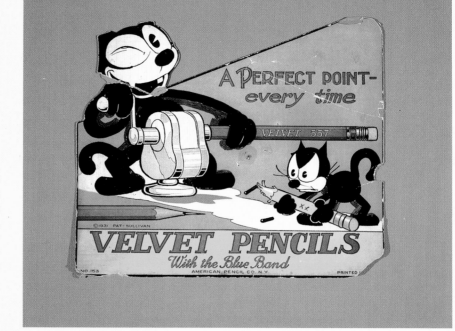

Marriner and the originator of a few minor strips of his own. He was an undistinguished draftsman with a rudimentary knowledge of animation learned on the job working for nine months with pioneer animator Raoul Barre, inventor of the peg system. In 1915, Sullivan opened his own studio, and used Universal's camera in Fort Lee to shoot animated advertising shorts and a series based on Marriner's strip.

Mayer and Sullivan both expressed to Jack Cohn an interest in working with the young man. ("Send that kid over to me," Mayer said, according to Messmer.) Given a choice between working with the little-known Sullivan and the famous Mayer, Messmer eagerly went to Hy Mayer, who he thought "had everything. He had been guest editor of London and Tokyo *Punch*. He was a friend of Teddy Roosevelt. He had souvenirs from all of them. And a giant studio, with a patio overlooking Central Park."

A Messmer cartoon in the *New York World* (*Fun* supplement), August 23, 1914. Courtesy Doris Messmer.

When they met at the cartoonist's apartment at 15 West Sixty-ninth Street, Mayer told Messmer, "I got a call to make an animated cartoon. I don't know anything about it, but you know a little bit about it." The film, *The Travels of Teddy*, which was really an elaborate commercial for the sponsor (Auerbach's Chocolates), starred a cartoon version of Mayer's friend Teddy Roosevelt. Messmer was delighted to assist Mayer, who "drew the key drawings, which was a crackerjack! He had a caricature of Roosevelt with the teeth, eyeglasses, helmet, and gun. All gags with elephants, different animals. Very clever guy. I moved them for him. He'd make the fellow at the start, but I could turn it around. I knew how to put the inbetweens [drawings between the main-action drawings] in. He was so delighted that it turned out great. That ran in theaters all over the country."

Messmer found working with Mayer a happy experience, one that gave him confidence. "I knew how to move 'em now," he said. Unemployed again, he decided to call on the other cartoonist who admired his drawings at Universal. This time Messmer's casual search for a job would change his life.

"I went to Pat Sullivan at 125 West Forty-second Street, right off Broadway. Just a dinky little room. He was just starting. That's the first time I met Sullivan."

DOWN UNDER

"WORK AND SOME IMAGINATION Make Good Cartoons"
is the headline of a small article in the April 29, 1916,
issue of *Motion Picture News*. The quotation, as well as
its placement in the trade journal, came from Pat Sullivan, "[who] has
been fashioning a number of animated cartoons for Universal which
have brought forth much favorable comment."

Thirty-one-year-old Sullivan was not, as Otto Messmer put it, "just
starting" in the animation field when they met in 1916; he was well
on his way. In less than two years, Sullivan—who was fired from his
first animation job in 1914 because his work was "unsatisfactory"—
had a distribution deal with a major company for a film series. The
cartoons starred "Sammy Johnsin," a black child adapted from a newspaper comic strip Sullivan had drawn for the McClure Syndicate.

Sullivan headed a small staff of artists who assisted him on the
Johnsin series, as well as created their own original animated shorts.
Sullivan took the animator's paper drawings, hired people to ink them
in, photographed them, and sold the films to various distributors. He
paid the artists, after taking a fee for his trouble and expenses.

The *Motion Picture News* piece is the earliest example of Sullivan's
keen instincts for self-promotion. Throughout his career, particularly
during Felix the Cat's heyday in the twenties, he used the print medium
to call attention to his work and his name, while deflecting information
about his personal life. Facts about Sullivan's earliest years are sketchy,
since much of what is known is based on self-serving newspaper interviews he gave late in his life. Often he mythologized his past, placing

Opposite: Two children play
with a large stuffed Felix doll
on an Australian beach, about
1925. Courtesy Bicentennial
Copying Project, State Library
of New South Wales.

it in a Horatio Alger light—i.e., a poor boy who made good abroad—glossing over difficulties he encountered in a relentless search for success. But there is enough information to piece together a chronology and to conclude that Sullivan's early years were never easy; they were, in fact, as he once bitterly described it, "a damned hard struggle."

Pat Sullivan's struggle began in Sydney, Australia, where he was born in 1885. Birth records for Sullivan do not exist; the date of 1885 is determined from Sullivan's 1933 death certificate and a New York City Magistrates Court statement in 1917.

The mideighties was a period of major expansion in the great port city, the oldest European settlement on the Australian continent, with a population of half a million.

Sullivan was born in the working-class suburb of Darlinghurst to Margaret and Patrick O'Sullivan. O'Sullivan, an Irishman, was said to be "Sydney's oldest cab driver." Pat and his older brother, William, used to watch his father and uncle, Bill Hayes, break horses in.

Pat enjoyed drawing as a child, but his mother tried to discourage him in favor of a career in music. "What's the use," she asked, "of drawing silly bits on a piece of paper?"

The Education Act of 1880 made it compulsory for children aged seven to fourteen years to attend school, so it is assumed Pat did. But school is never mentioned in his later publicity, although boyhood activities are, such as producing a "newspaper" he called *Blowflies* with neighborhood chums. One of the kids, Tom Doyle, who later became Secretary of the United Labourer's Union, told how he, Pat, and William O'Sullivan earned "many a bob" singing outside hotels.

His early attempts to find work in the cartoon field resulted in dropping the "O" from his surname, a 1925 Australian newspaper clipping explains:

> In the old days when Pasquin, the Sydney caricaturist familiarly known as "PAS," and Pat were struggling for a crust, they used to contribute sketches to the press under the respective pen-names of PO's and PAS. The two names became a riddle to editors. PAS rejects were mailed back to PO's and vice versa until Pat O'Sullivan became Pat Sullivan to obviate the difficulty.

Pat Sullivan (left), with his father, Patrick O'Sullivan, and brother, William J. O'Sullivan, of Sydney, Australia. Courtesy Doris Messmer.

"The happiest moment of my life," Pat once told a reporter, "was when my first cartoons were published."

Sullivan eventually drew the occasional cartoon for *The Worker*, a labor weekly. For one assignment he illustrated a story by James S. Ryan, who years later penned a letter of support on behalf of Sullivan in a time of trouble. Sullivan's drawings, Ryan wrote, "were so unique that I sought him out, and we became well acquainted. I found him a kindly young fellow always willing to assist a brother artist who happened to be down on his luck. Bohemia can offer no better tribute to the character of a man than to say that he was unselfish at the same time that he had great possibilities as a comic artist . . . his achievements were the results of . . . his own talent, energy, and perseverance against terrific odds in Australia, England and the United States."

A search through 150 issues of *The Gadfly*, a "society/gossip/humour" weekly published between 1906 and 1909 in Adelaide, South Australia, found only one cartoon by Pat Sullivan: in the June 19, 1907, issue a spot illustration appears in which a nervous female passenger on a ship asks a pipe-smoking seaman if there is "any fear of drowning?" To which the sailor replies no, because "this place is full of sharks." The drawing is painfully amateurish and poorly composed, the woman seeming to disappear in the detailed ocean wave behind her and the sailor tilted off-balance.

In 1907, when he was twenty-two years old, Sullivan left Australia, hoping to better his luck in London. "Australia was too far from the center of things," the *Peoria Sunday Morning Star* explained in an article on Sullivan on April 5, 1931, "so when Pat graduated to long pants he kissed the kangaroo country toodleoo and boarded a boat for London."

Christmas, 1907! Left: Pat. O'Sulli- van, of Felix the Cat fame; Right: Mr. T. D. Mutch, Minister for Edu- cation. A couple of Sydney lads who made good.

A photo of Pat Sullivan (left) and friend T. D. Mutch in Sydney at Christmastime, 1907, published in the December 18, 1925, Sydney *Daily Guardian*.

Sullivan's luck during his brief stay in London was dismal. "As a matter of fact," he said years later, "I actually starved." Penniless and homeless, his bed was often the Thames embankment. When he managed to sell drawings in Fleet Street for a few shillings each, he found humble lodgings in South London. "In one of them," recalled Sullivan, "my landlady used to drink my whiskey when I was out. So I wrote the word 'poison' in large letters on the label. But she still went on drinking the whiskey. I found out, afterwards, that she could not read." It is ironic that the first public association of Sullivan and alcohol is an anecdote he told on himself.

After a series of disappointments, Sullivan finally got a job doing cartoons for a comic journal. In his own words, he was "a no-account sort of comic artist. . . . I did drawings which editors were occasionally kind enough to buy from me at two shillings each." He managed to sell some cartoons to the humorous weeklies *Ally Sloper* and *Sketchy Bits*, and newspapers such as the *Bulletin* and *London Daily Mail*.

"The return in pounds sterling wasn't quite enough to satisfy the cartoonist, so he tried his hand at the theatrical game," reports the 1931 *Peoria Star*. "Sullivan appeared in London music halls doing a dance and song act." His partner in the act was a British fellow named George Clardey, who later became an animator at Sullivan's first studio in New York. "Sullivan would come out [on stage]," said Messmer, "and he would draw a face. They had some trick where Clardey on the other side [of the drawing board]—the face would animate. They would substitute a red balloon [for a nose]. Blow it up." "The fact that he is still alive," opined a London newspaper years later about the Sullivan-Clardey performance, "testifies that he wasn't as bad as some might think. Anyone who can live through a London music hall is fairly good."

"The try at acting wasn't so successful," according to the *Peoria Star*, "and he turned to the exhibiting end of the game, being one of the pioneer motion picture exhibitors in England. In spite of plenty of hard work this business wasn't a financial success. Mr. Sullivan dropped it." A London paper put it more bluntly: "Pat sank lower and lower in the social scale by becoming a movie picture exhibitor . . . but his fate was that of the majority of pioneers—he went broke."

Sullivan, the erstwhile cartoonist, performer, and movie exhibitor, was now in desperate straits, the depths of which are indicated by his next job: "He hired himself out as a gentleman in waiting and special valet to a boat load of mules." For a year, (probably on and off) Sullivan traveled back and forth across the Atlantic feeding and tending Missouri mules, who were "well pleased with his butlering." On a docking at New York harbor in 1909, Sullivan jumped ship.

In 1925, in London for a grand Felix publicity tour, successful and wealthy Pat Sullivan explained his decision to stay in the United States with elegant understatement: "As fortune did not smile on me here," he said, "I went to New York."

Drawn for The Gadfly *by Pat Sullivan.*

A rare example of Sullivan's early published work, from the Australian "society/gossip/humour" weekly *The Gadfly*. Courtesy David Watson.

25

"PHYSICUL JOGRAPHY" Taught By Experience

COMIC STRIP TO COMIC SCREEN, 1909–1916

NEW YORK did not welcome Pat Sullivan any more warmly than London or Sydney. So the twenty-four-year-old Sullivan, grown "hard and strong" from transatlantic mule tending, tried yet another career path. "Having had to rap the mules when they got unruly, Pat developed quite a right cross to the chin," according to the April 5, 1931, *Peoria Star*. "So Mr. Sullivan figured he could make more money slapping down humans in America. He . . . took up the none too gentle art of fisticuffing. After tucking the scalps of a few lightweights under his belt, Mr. Sullivan decided pugilism was not in his line. The urge to draw began to make itself felt within himself again. . . ."

Another account indicates it was self-preservation that put an end to Sullivan's brief foray into boxing: "A couple of left wings to the button, however, convinced him that pugilism wasn't his main forte, and that the pen is mightier than the five-ounce glove."

In 1911, Sullivan's luck finally began to change for the better when his "drawing urge" somehow led him to the McClure Newspaper Syndicate. According to comic-strip historian Mark Johnson, the T. C. McClure company was launched in 1901 and "several big time newspapers picked up this new section for the first several months, but soon dropped them for other options, other syndicates or their own homemade job. No paper, for the next 25 years, ever held on to a McClure section for very long. None of it was really hot stuff. Everybody would rather have had Hearst's comic section."

During his on-and-off three-year tenure at McClure's, Sullivan was

Opposite: *Sambo and His Funny Noises*, a Sunday comic strip by William F. Marriner. This late example from the October 11, 1914, *Milwaukee Free Press* may have been drawn by Marriner's assistant, Pat Sullivan. Collection of Mark Johnson.

one of a number of assistants to cartoonist William F. Marriner on his comic strip *Sambo and His Funny Noises*. Marriner was a popular cartoonist whose one-panel spot gags appeared in the earliest comic sections: in Pulitzer's papers in 1897 and in Hearst's as far back as 1896. He was also a contributor to *Life*, the humor magazine, in 1897.

By early 1905, the prolific Marriner was at work for McClure, doing a standard hobo strip—*Glad Rags, the Corpulant* [sic] *Tramp*—an idea which, says Johnson, "was used thousands of times in those years by lazy cartoonists," and *Wags, the Dog That Adopted a Man*, about a canine that brings bad luck to his would-be owners.

Many of Marriner's works are unsigned, but his stylistic signature—oval, catatonic eyes in large, hydrocephaloid heads atop tiny bodies and oversized shoes—is easily recognizable in a number of his strips and spot drawings featuring boy protagonists, e.g., *Captain Kidde, Hys Cheste*, Benny Brown, Willie White, Bobby Black from the *Kidde* series, *Little Willie and Cousin Jerry, Fortunes of Foolish Ferdinand, Billy Blinks, the Boy Burglar*, and Marriner's most popular McClure strip, *Sambo and His Funny Noises*, first published in 1905.

"Kid strips" were extremely popular during the first part of this century, starting with R. F. Outcault's Yellow Kid and Buster Brown, and including among others Winsor McCay's Little Nemo, James Swinnerton's Jimmy, and Rudolph Dirks's Katzenjammer Kids. Marriner, in search of a variation on yet another of his kid strips, was no doubt influenced by the famous children's book *Little Black Sambo*, by Helen Bannerman, written in 1899. By using a black child named "Sambo" as the strip's protagonist, Marriner profited from the popularity of the book. Also "Sambo" was already in general usage as a put-down for black males.

Marriner's Sambo is a poor street kid, drawn with the usual large head with wide oval eyes on a tiny body. His peers look the same, except that Sambo is drawn with heavy cross-hatching to indicate he is black, and he has thick lips. He also wears a hat perched so far on the side of his head as to defy gravity and so small it looks like a sink plug.

The "funny noises" of the strip's title refers to what Sambo says (in a thick dialect) and does. His penchant for distorting the truth sometimes enables him to triumph over his white chums and win their grudging respect. But usually, he is verbally or (more often) physically attacked.

One of the saddest and most chillingly racist *Sambo* strips appeared in the December 7, 1913, *San Francisco Chronicle*. It begins with Sambo joyously announcing to the world at large: "Hooray! Hooray! I'se ten yeahs ole to-day!" His happiness is short-lived as five white boys grab him and beat him ten times with a wooden board. Sambo amends his former announcement: "I isent ten. I'se only five yeahs old," which leads to a beating of only five whacks. And so Sambo learns. He reduces the fact of his birth even more radically and silently carries a sign through the neighborhood that reads:

NOTICE
Dis aint my birfday
I neber had no birfday
I don't want no birfday
So fergit it
s. Jonsin esq

"Now! Maybe dey'll lemme alone awhile," mumbles Sambo, who, in order to survive in the white man's world, has learned to deny his very existence.

Pat Sullivan was well chosen as an assistant to Marriner in that their graphic style was similar and both men were fond of the bottle. For the McClure Syndicate, Sullivan also created a few of his own short-lived strips, such as *Willing Waldo—He Wants Work* and *Old Pop Perkins*. The latter strip was signed by Sullivan, and so it affords us a definite example of his drawing style and humor at this period of his career. Old Pop is a standard "geezer" character, an oldster who speaks his mind no matter the consequences. Public officials and city slickers usually bear the brunt of Pop's innocently spoken remarks. In the January 31, 1915, *St. Louis Republic*, it is a top-hatted, fast-talking cigar salesman who is stung. Sullivan's pen line is thin, his characters circular, the action minimal, and the staging stilted. Walking characters are usually shown in extreme profile, one foot thrust forward. A slight variation is used to simulate the agitated movements of a chase:

WILLING WALDO — HE WANTS WORK

characters in profile, both legs spread wide, with action lines and dust and sweat symbols to indicate speed and exertion. Backgrounds are simple, often containing a tilted line to represent a landscape that holds a tree or, more often, a triangle-roofed house with a line of smoke curling out of a chimney.

Sullivan's salary at McClure's never averaged more than forty-five dollars per week, but the work was easier than punching mules (or men, for that matter). To make extra money, Sullivan's entrepreneurial qualities began to come to the fore. According to Hal Walker, Sullivan was a good salesman who convinced known cartoonists to draw some of his ideas for a series of postcards that he had printed and sold. One of the surviving postcards carries a copyright symbol for the "Unique Pub. Co, N.Y. 1911" but no artist's signature. It is not Sullivan's hand, however, judging from examples of his broad cartoon style. The drafts-

"OLD POP PERKINS"

manship is too detailed and tends toward naturalism, with shadows and gray tones throughout. The postcard is of the "naughty" traveling salesman variety, a sexist joke on a waitress whose ample buttocks push against the table of a portly man in a loud checkered coat. Inspired by the pulchritudinous "hen"/"chick"/"bird" before him, the man winks to the waiter as he stretches his chubby hand toward the woman and changes his food order from beef to chicken.

On Friday, October 9, 1914, William Marriner's charred remains were found in the ruins of his summer home at Harrington Park near Hackensack, New Jersey. According to the police report, detectives originally thought Marriner, who suffered a gunshot wound, was "murdered by a burglar who burned the house to hide his crime" (*New York Times*, October 11, 1914). But their theory changed to suicide when a neighbor reported that "Marriner was under the influence of liquor on

Two strips created and drawn by Pat Sullivan: *Willing Waldo* (*St. Paul Sunday Pioneer Press*, November 2, 1913) and *Old Pop Perkins* (*St. Louis Republic*, January 31, 1915). Collection of Mark Johnson.

31

Thursday afternoon . . . and when I stopped to speak to him, he said: 'If my wife doesn't come home tonight, I'll burn my house and the whole village.' It is said that Mrs. Marriner always went to New York when her husband began to drink."

After Marriner's death, Sullivan continued to ghost *Sambo* for a brief time, but without Marriner to write and supervise it, the strip terminated at year's end. Sullivan was no doubt aware of the successful transfer of the comic strips of Winsor McCay and George McManus from the page to the screen and he envisioned a similar fate for *Sambo*. In order to learn the craft of animation, Sullivan used his persuasive salesmanship to obtain on-the-job training. By spring of 1915, he was making five dollars less per week than he did at McClure's at one of the earliest animation studios, Raoul Barre's Animated Cartoons, Inc., in the Fordham section of the Bronx.

Raoul Barre is an important but unsung animation innovator. A French Canadian who drew the first Québecois comic strip, Barre saw his first animated cartoon—perhaps Winsor McCay's *How a Mosquito Operates*—when he moved to New York in 1912. Barre decided to get into the animation business, and visited the Edison studios in Fort Lee, New Jersey, to learn more about how to make drawings move.

He found out that McCay's drawing style and techniques were too time-consuming to be profitable. So, with William C. Nolan, who shot live-action advertisements on Edison's equipment, Barre devised a number of methods to streamline production for a series of animated cartoons. Barre's innovations included tearing the paper around a character to allow the background (on a separate paper underneath) to show through. This slash-and-tear method did away with the need to tediously copy the stationary background on each drawing, as McCay did.

In order to accurately register the animation drawings one on top of the other, Barre improved on McCay's use of crosses in the corners of his drawings. Barre punched holes at the top of the papers and placed them over fixed pegs on the drawing board.

John Randolph Bray, another cartoonist inspired by the popularity of the films of pioneer animators J. S. Blackton, Emile Cohl, and Winsor McCay, also searched for ways to ease the labor of animation in order to make it profitable. In 1914, Bray patented (with animator Earl Hurd) a method using celluloid acetate, or "cels," to separate the multiple character drawings from a stationary background. Bray's cels and Barre's pegs remain the dominant production methods used in today's animation studios.

Bray and Barre were professional rivals, and each claimed to have established the first animation studio in 1913. Barre's studio was, according to veteran animator I. Klein, "a long ride up the old, now long demolished, Third Avenue Elevated line (the El) to its last stop, Fordham Road, Bronx Park. . . . No high-rise buildings were on 190th Street and Webster Avenue. The studio was in a long, low building called Fordham Arcade Building. A row of stores with one floor of offices above. The architecture was bastard Moorish. . . . An arcaded passage-way ran through from Webster Avenue to Decatur Avenue in the back." Upstairs and down a long hallway, Klein entered a door with Barre's name on it and found himself in a room with rows of men working at animation light tables. "Though this was a sunny day, the room was in twilight gloom. This dimness was due to the green paint which covered the studio windows. A glow of light illuminated a face here and there from the animation boards."

One of a series of postcards produced, but not drawn, by Pat Sullivan in 1911. Collection of Hal Walker.

Sullivan was learning on the job with Gregory La Cava, Bill Nolan, and Frank Moser on a series for Edison called the *Animated Grouch Chaser*. The series is basically live-action with inserts of animation; in *Cartoons on the Beach*, for example, a group of young women and men in tank-top swimsuits pass the time reading comic-book pages that come to life in animation. "Come to life" is too generous a description, for most of the character's movements are extremely limited, badly timed, and ineptly staged. However, a full array of state-of-the-art animation techniques circa 1915 is observable in the *Grouch Chaser* series, including slash-and-tear, cels, cutouts, cycles (repetition of drawings), and background pans. But the films are obviously the work of several hands, as there is little consistency in drawing styles even within the animated segments, and some animation gags work better than others because certain of the animators were more skilled than others. To modern eyes, Barre's early work looks haphazard and crude (to correctly use a word that is often overused when describing pre-Disney animation).

It was a time of self-discovery and groping in the dark; Winsor McCay's beautifully drawn films, meticulously made by himself over lengthy periods of time, were not an easy act to follow. "From a distance, what these men achieved may not seem impressive," wrote critic André Martin in 1976 in a sympathetic appraisal of Barre and his studio, "but in fact they created a graphic and dynamic system of representation without precedent . . . the artists of the New York school of animation, in the anonymity of their studios, had to construct from nothing a precise craft, and to resolve a whole series of fundamental problems in the areas of structure and form; notably inking the outline, careful superimposition of the different animated phases during the drawing and shooting, insertion of backgrounds and half-tones."

It is significant that even at the Barre studio, Pat Sullivan's talent was considered inferior. After only nine months, he was, in fact, "laid off as his work was unsatisfactory." It is also significant that the firing did not stop Sullivan, but perhaps emboldened him to open his own animation shop. After all, he had soaked up much information during his brief time at Barre's; the animation game didn't seem so difficult, as long as you got a number of talented people to do the laborious parts. It is a measure of the man's resourcefulness and will to survive

PAT SULLIVAN ·
ANIMATED CARTOONS
125 WEST 42 ST
NEW···YORK

The 1915 business envelope for
Pat Sullivan's studio. Collection
of Leslie Carbaga.

that by mid-1915 Sullivan was at work in his own studio at 121 West
Forty-second Street.

By the time Otto Messmer met him in early 1916, Sullivan had
moved next door to 125 West Forty-second Street, and had contracts
with the Efanem Film Company and the Edison Company for advertising and split-reel entertainment shorts. He even followed through
with his idea to turn the *Sambo* strip into animation. Renamed *Sammy
Johnsin* to avoid litigation from Marriner's heirs, the film series starring
the little black boy was produced by Pat Powers and released by
Universal.

Sullivan was only seven years Messmer's senior, but in terms of
worldly experience he was light-years ahead. The two young men were
total opposites: Sullivan was outgoing and earthy, Messmer soft-spoken
and reticent. Sullivan had traveled around the globe and led a colorful
life; Messmer still lived with his parents in New Jersey. Sullivan assisted a famous newspaper cartoonist, took over his well-known comic
strip, and created his own strips; Messmer sold spot cartoons to a few
newspapers and magazines. Messmer had made only two animated
films, one of them as the anonymous assistant to Hy Mayer; Sullivan
ran his own studio with a staff turning out a series of films under his
name and was making his mark as a producer with bold, sure strokes.

Messmer admired Sullivan "cause his stuff was goin' pretty good.
And I was very thankful to him to give me the start [*sic*]." Sullivan,
for his part, knew a useful talent when he saw one. Messmer didn't

need be taught how to animate from scratch like so many of the cartoonists Sullivan was hiring; he merely required a bit of polishing and an explanation of how animated films were made in the big studios, like Barre's.

"I give [Sullivan] great credit," said Messmer. "He taught me a lot of things about timing, so forth. He began to get a few other fellas, and we each made our own conception, any creation that came into our minds, and he would sell it." Messmer recalled the studio was "not too big. We still didn't have a camera. It was about eight men. There were two or three of them I don't think they ever completed anything." Some of the names of cartoonists who passed through Sullivan's at this time include Charles Saxon, Will Anderson, William Stark, Charles Santon, R. Eggeman, W. E. Stork, Bill Cause, and Arthur T. Crichton. Two of the cartoonists were men Sullivan first met in Britain: Ernest Smythe and George Clardey, his partner in his short-lived London music hall act.

Few women worked in the male-dominated field of animation, except to fill in the outlines of characters with black ink. According to Messmer, Sullivan "had a few girls here to process [the drawings], blacken [them] in." Mildred Walker may have been one of the so-called blackeners, although a trade magazine, *Motion Picture News* of April 29, 1916, described her as "another artist on the Sullivan staff" who "has just entered the field, and Mr. Sullivan is exploiting her work, the first of which will appear shortly." Nothing more is known of Walker's work or the woman herself, except that in 1917 she was a witness at Pat Sullivan's hasty marriage.

Historian Donald Crafton estimates nine *Sammy Johnsin* shorts and some independent shorts by Messmer were released between March and December 1916. Among the several short-lived characters turned out at Sullivan's were *Fearless Freddie* and *Willie Slate* (from Messmer); *Willie Winks* (which sprang solely from Sullivan's pencil); and *Boomer Bill*, *Boxcar Bill*, and *Hardrock Dome* (from unknown others). In December, Sullivan released a Messmer cartoon called *Trials of a Movie Cartoonist* through distributor Pat Powers. This now lost film's content predicts the format of Max Fleischer's *Out of the Inkwell* cartoons, which appeared three years later. The December 9, 1916,

Opposite: The *Sambo* strip of July 15, 1906, in the Columbus, Ohio, *Press-Post*, a newspaper whose masthead motto was "With a mission and without a muzzle." Collection of Mark Johnson.

Moving Picture World describes the film as depicting the "tribulations of a movie cartoonist at work. The figures he draws become rebellious and refuse to act as he wants them to, so he has a terrible time to make them do his bidding. They answer back and say he has no right to make slaves of them even if he is their creator."

In addition to one-shot productions and the *Sammy Johnsin* series, Sullivan and staff also produced a dozen *Charlie Chaplin* cartoons in 1916. The idea for the series came from a Mr. Fiedler of Empire City Laboratory who sold the idea to Chaplin and then approached Sullivan. "So Chaplin sent at least thirty or forty photographs of himself in different [poses]," said Messmer. "He was delighted, cause this helped the propagation of his pictures, ya see? And he encouraged us and autographed all these photographs and we copied every little movement that he did."

Just as the little black boy, Sammy Johnsin, would later affect the look of the future Felix the Cat, the Chaplin cartoon series proved to have a profound effect on Felix's subtle pantomimic behavior and facial expressions. "Later that rubbed off and we used a lot of that kind of action in Felix," said Messmer. "We thought a funny walk sometimes would get a laugh without [a] script idea. Or the wiggling of the tail, things of that type. . . . Chaplin had a great influence on us."

"I don't want to praise myself," said the ever modest Messmer, "I got pretty efficient at it. I learned. Was ambitious." He became fast with a pencil, turning out more film footage than his colleagues. Messmer also tried to "make a thing that would make people laugh, instead of just makin' them move." He added gags to standard chase scenes in the *Sammy Johnsin* series: "Funny little things Sambo would do. If a lion was chasin' him, his hat would blow off, and then when he would stop the hat would come on him again. Little things like that."

Messmer was beginning to develop a personal philosophy regarding the proper use of animation as opposed to live-action. "I went for simplicity," he said, "and I didn't try to make human beings. How can you get a laugh out of that? Chaplin and the real Keystone Kops did everything possible."

Let Barre have his Mutt and Jeff, Bray his Colonel Heeza Liar, and Earl Hurd his Bobby Bumps—all human characters that moved in mundane, predictable ways. "Why animate something that you can see in real life?" said Messmer. "Some [animators] tried to make beautiful girls moving around, and men. It didn't go over too well with audiences in theaters. But if they saw even a rubber ball with a face on it—a drawing moving, doing things—it got a thrill."

Otto Messmer decided to stake a claim for the impossible in animation whenever he could. He would celebrate the cartoon *as* cartoon, as something totally removed from reality. He would create simple symbols of animal characters, who would in turn make brilliant use of metamorphosis—animation's intrinsic, magical property, which live-action cannot duplicate.

DERAILMENT, 1917–1919

NINETEEN HUNDRED AND SEVENTEEN promised to be an even more successful year for Pat Sullivan and his studio than the previous year. "One of the big things we did," said Otto Messmer, was to create a prologue to Universal's feature *Twenty Thousand Leagues Under the Sea*. The two-reel short, commissioned by Universal, was given the parodic title *Twenty Thousand Laughs Under the Sea*.

Increasingly occupied with business details, Sullivan began to delegate more and more creative responsibility to Messmer. "I did it all practically by myself," said Messmer of *Twenty Thousand Laughs*. "I dashed through that. I had a fellow, a little character . . . a dog or something. He had a barrel, a little stovepipe on top for a periscope, and he went down [under the sea]." Some of the gags included "a bunch of fish gettin' soused at the sand bar . . . pickled herring. A school of fish with kids playing hooky. Then there was a dragon with legs marching endless. Twenty thousand legs under the sea, we called that."

Observing audience reactions in the theater, Messmer saw his visual puns and outlandish gags "went over really well. I mean it really got some laughs. I learned from this that people laugh mostly when you did something that's impossible."

In 1917, Messmer and Sullivan were dating the women who would become their wives. Messmer first met Anne Mason, elegant daughter of a Scottish plasterer, in 1912 at Midland Beach on Staten Island. The couple would remain true to each each other for over seventy-one years, including fifty-nine years of marriage.

Opposite: A Pat Sullivan drawing on the envelope of a letter sent from jail to his lawyer on August 19, 1917. Courtesy Estate of Harry Kopp.

Otto Messmer and his future wife, Anne Mason, at Midland Beach, Staten Island, in 1912. Courtesy Doris Messmer.

Pat Sullivan dated a number of women and entertained them in the furnished apartment at 10 Manhattan Avenue near 100th Street that he began renting in May. But 1917 Manhattan District Attorney records quote Wilmot Craven, the apartment building's elevator boy and switchboard operator, as saying he "brought one girl in steadily all the time," a certain "Miss Thomas," who "came in there and stayed all night with him."

Sullivan's steady girlfriend was vivacious twenty-nine-year-old Margaret (Marjorie) Gallagher, who used the surname of her first husband, J. J. Thomas, as her maiden name. She was one of seven daughters and two sons born to Thomas and Sarah Gallagher of Scranton, Pennsylvania.

When Marjorie left Scranton for New York is not known, nor is there information about her first marriage. How she met Pat Sullivan is also a mystery, although Otto Messmer recalled she was one of the Sullivan studio's female inkers: "We had quite a few inkers there. [She was] very young, very jovial. [He] had a lot of girls [for inking]. Took a whole day to blacken in [the cartoon characters]."

What *is* certain is the date of Marjorie and Pat Sullivan's marriage— May 21, 1917—which occurred hurriedly and during one of the darkest episodes of Sullivan's life. Sullivan's time of professional and personal upheaval began innocently enough.

On Friday, April 27, two teenage girls from Rutherford, New Jersey, Alice McCleary and Gladys Bowen, rented a room at 132 West Forty-third Street. Dark-haired Alice, age fourteen, and her blond friend, Gladys, age fifteen, were having an adventure. Five days before, they had run away from their homes with vague plans to go on the stage.

From the window of their furnished room, they could look over a backyard into the fourth-floor window in the back of the building at 125 West Forty-second Street. There, they saw a group of men working at light tables, two of whom, Ernest Smythe and Pat Sullivan, noticed the girls, who began to flirt.

After much waving and winking, Smythe motioned to the giggling girls to come downstairs. Gladys went and returned with an invitation to meet Smythe and Sullivan that evening. At 9:00 P.M., the two men took the girls to a café down the block from their rooming house at the corner of Sixth Avenue and Forty-third Street. After Sullivan ordered creme-de-menthes for himself and the girls, and a beer for Smythe, the men told the teenagers "they were artists and were employed making cartoons for 'animated pictures'." After an hour, the girls returned to their rooming house.

The next evening, a Saturday, Sullivan and Smythe took the girls back to the saloon, ordered a couple of rounds of creme-de-menthes, then taxied fifty-seven blocks uptown to Sullivan's apartment at 10 Manhattan Avenue.

After some sherry and heavy petting, Alice and Gladys were escorted back to their lodgings by Smythe, while Sullivan went elsewhere. But not before Alice promised to meet Sullivan the next night.

At 8:00 P.M. on Sunday, Pat Sullivan arrived to pick up fourteen-year-old Alice for a solo date. She hesitated to go with him, but he urged her in the presence of Gladys, telling her she would come to no harm. Leaving Gladys at the stoop of the rooming house, Alice and Pat boarded the Sixth Avenue elevated train for the long ride to Sullivan's apartment.

On May 10, Pat Sullivan and Ernest Smythe were placed under arrest by Officer Cooper of New York's Detective Bureau and Special Officer Juan Butts of the New York Society for the Prevention of Cruelty to Children (SPCC). Smythe was charged with "abduction," which was later changed to a lesser complaint of "impairing morals." Sullivan, however, was charged with the rape of an underage female.

It was the actions of George Clardey, Sullivan's employee and former vaudeville partner, that led to Sullivan's arrest and ultimately his conviction. At the studio the morning after his evening with Alice McCleary, Sullivan had bragged to Clardey that "he had screwed the dark one."

Clardey was determined "to get the girls away from [Sullivan] and his friends." He arranged for the teenagers to speak with an acquaintance of his, Julia Siggins, a moving picture actress. Horrified by their story, Mrs. Siggins immediately took charge. She found new lodging for the girls with a Mrs. B. Leo on Seventh Avenue, jobs at a "5 and 10 cents store," and supplied them with clean, "plain dresses." She also "noticed some suspicious stains on Alice's clothing and, believing the child had contracted a disease from [Sullivan]," she turned the clothes over to detectives and confronted the cartoonist. This is the first of a number of persistent indications that Sullivan suffered from a venereal disease.

Sullivan was released from jail on $2,500 bail, and eleven days after his arrest he married Marjorie Gallagher on May 21 at Manhattan's Municipal Building.

The next day, Sullivan was indicted on a charge of "rape in the second degree," convicted after a jury trial on June 21, and finally sentenced on September 13. From the time of the indictment to sentencing, Sullivan was jailed in the city prison known as the Tombs. He spent such a lengthy time there after the trial ended because his lawyer, Harry Kopp, needed time to "prepare papers for an application for a new trial [based] on alleged newly discovered evidence."

Kopp was the second (and final) lawyer retained by Sullivan to argue his case, and he remained Sullivan's attorney, agent, and friend until the cartoonist's death in 1933. Born in Brest-Litovsk, Russia, in 1880, Kopp was a cigar-chomping, blunt-spoken asthmatic, whose chronic ill-health did not prevent him from "speaking his mind on any subject" or becoming, in the opinion of more than one of his peers, a terrific trial lawyer.

Kopp filed a motion dated August 29, 1917, to set aside the conviction judgment rendered against Pat Sullivan on the ground of newly discovered evidence. The motion for a new trial was denied, for "in the opinion of the Court, the verdict of the jury was justified by the evidence" and the "alleged facts" in affidavits made in support of a new trial "would not, had they been presented at the trial, have changed the result" of the case.

Judge Crain took into account that Sullivan was "a man of very considerable ability" who was "without criminal record." He also acknowledged receiving a number of letters "from reputable people who speak well of you." He agreed that Sullivan had been "punished by the imprisonment which you have undergone between the date of your conviction and this day . . . [and] although that confinement was really at your own request, [it] ought to be taken into consideration in the imposition of sentence." The maximum penalty under the law for a

Harry Kopp, Pat Sullivan's attorney. Courtesy Estate of Harry Kopp.

Opposite: A letter from Marjorie Gallagher Sullivan to Judge C. T. Crain dated September 12, 1917, the day before her husband, Pat Sullivan, was sentenced. Courtesy City of New York Municipal Archives.

PAT SULLIVAN
ANIMATED . CARTOONS
125 WEST 42ST
NEW . YORK . CITY .

TEL
1382
BRYANT

Wes - 12 - 17

Hon C. I Crain
    Dear Sir;
            Just a line asking
you if you will be as lenient
with my husbands sentence
(Pat Sullivan) as possible, for
I know if any one knows he
is inocent of this crime.
        Trusting you will listen to my
plea and down in my heart I ask
this only favor
            Truly yours
            Mrs Pat Sullivan

person convicted of rape in the second degree was imprisonment for not more than ten years; Judge Crain sentenced Sullivan to the Sing Sing State Prison in Ossining, New York, "for not less than one year and not more than two."

Sullivan was permitted to draw in prison, but he could do very little animation alone, and so his film contracts dried up and his staff drifted to other jobs.

Messmer continued to contribute gag cartoons to periodicals, including *Life*, the prestigious humor magazine. His decorative drawing style was now more confident, his character designs as witty as ever and perfectly arranged, e.g., the "Musically Inclined" anatomically twisted horn player in the October 4, 1917, issue and the rounded farmer peacefully resting with his "Back to Nature" in the July 12, 1917, issue.

Messmer also returned to work for Hy Mayer, who was starting his own studio. "He always wanted to do that and he put me in charge of it," said Messmer. Mayer hired several cartoonists who had been with

An illustrated letter dated August 19, 1917, sent by Pat Sullivan from the New York City jail known as the Tombs to his lawyer, Harry Kopp. Courtesy Estate of Harry Kopp.

"It does'nt take some lawyers long to dispose of a case,"

the Sullivan studio, "practically the whole gang," recalled Messmer. But America entered World War I in 1917, and a number of Mayer's staff were drafted, including Otto Messmer. "So I had to leave," he lamented. "Just when I was starting to sell like mad cartoons to the magazines."

Messmer was one of a number of men slotted for "heavy training" as a telegraph operator in the 104th Field Signal Corps at Camp McClellan in Anniston, Alabama. On June 19, he sailed from Hoboken, New Jersey, aboard the S.S. *Great Northern* headed for France.

Messmer witnessed his share of horrors. He recalled speaking with a buddy in the trenches one moment, then turning to discover a bullet hole had pierced the man's head. Then there was a German sniper shot out of a tree, who conversed with Messmer in German as he lay dying. The man showed the American soldiers pictures of his wife and children, and offered them cigarettes and candies.

Messmer's buddies in the corps didn't believe him when he told them "he had drawn the Sammy Johnsin and Charlie Chaplin cartoons that were projected evenings." Only after his girlfriend, Anne, sent him one of his *Life* cartoons signed "Otz Messmer" were they convinced "that he was perhaps not a liar after all."

On May 28, 1919, Messmer finally returned home. He discovered Pat Sullivan "was out of 'the war,' too." Sullivan, in fact, served only nine months of his jail sentence and had been back at his Forty-second Street studio for almost a year. (As a convicted felon, he would not have been draft-eligible.)

A small notice in the trade journal *Motion Picture News* of July 6, 1918, announced Sullivan's return to "Cartoon Making":

[He] is at present engaged in completing a thousand foot subject of the war, a humorous conceit in which the Kaiser figures in the heavy role. The channel of release for this subject will be announced shortly.

Mr. Sullivan also has a good two hundred pounds of finished drawings in his office which he will shortly start photographing. The two hundred pounds represents 8,500 complete drawings and when these are properly photographed he will have produced a three thousand foot animated cartoon. When this is completed it will be the longest animated cartoon ever produced. The majority of them run between five hundred and a thousand feet. Mr. Sullivan is negotiating with several companies regarding the release of this subject.

Private Otto Messmer in France in 1918. Courtesy Doris Messmer.

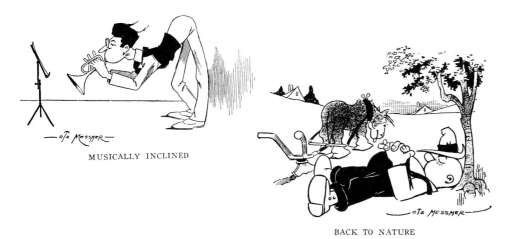

MUSICALLY INCLINED

BACK TO NATURE

Two Messmer gag cartoons from *Life*, the humor magazine: (left) October 4, 1917, and (right) July 12, 1917. Courtesy Doris Messmer.

The self-promotional article is vague about Sullivan's film plans; it mentions no distributors by name or release dates. It does indicate Sullivan was hopeful and "enthusiastic regarding his return to the business." Not mentioned, of course, was where Sullivan had returned from or the reason he went away. Curiously, Sullivan's rape charge and his imprisonment, although gossiped about within the industry for years, were never mentioned in print during his lifetime.

The *Motion Picture News* article emphasized that Sullivan had "already gained a reputation as [a] producer of animated cartoons," and as would later happen with the Felix series, he took full credit for "having drawn and animated the 'Sammie [*sic*] Johnsin' series for the Universal program."

Sullivan was holding on, working only with his wife, trying to sell full-reel cartoons here and there, trying to get things going. When Messmer rejoined Sullivan, the animation chores were once again in good hands, so Sullivan could concentrate on drumming up work. They started to make Chaplin cartoons again, and animated short parodies of travelogues for Triangle Films. The little studio became so busy in 1919 that when Earl Hurd, who put together the animation sections of the *Paramount Screen Magazine* (a weekly news-travelogue-cartoon compilation that accompanied a feature film), asked the Sullivan studio to fill in for a tardy animator, Sullivan almost said no.

But a job was a job, and he told Messmer, "If you want to do it on the side, you can do any little thing to satisfy them." At home in New Jersey, nights and on weekends, Messmer made animated drawings in pencil, then brought them to the studio to "a couple of girls who inked and blackened it in." To save time and labor, he decided to make the film's protagonist, a cat, all black "because it saves making a lot of outlines, and solid black moves better."

Audiences liked the Messmer-Sullivan cat film, which was called *Feline Follies*, so Paramount decided they liked it, too. "They ordered another one and another one. Then finally, a whole series." Silently, on little cat paws, the phenomenon soon to be known as Felix the Cat had arrived.

THE COMING OF THE CAT, 1919–1921

SULLIVAN AND MESSMER'S contribution to the *Paramount Screen Magazine* contained no known characters. Nor was their film the most beautifully drawn and animated; there was no competing in that department with Frank Moser, whose skillful technique ranged from naturalistic human and animal movements to convincing special effects, such as storms at sea. "Moser was one of those guys," recalled Messmer, "who did magnificent animation. But no laughs. But you had to admire his stuff."

Laughter was what the Messmer-Sullivan film offered audiences, laughter based on surprising visual gags and the delightful pantomime performance of a scruffy-looking black cat.

Many of the motifs used through the years to represent the world of Felix the Cat and his personality appear full-blown in his four-minute, ten-second debut film, *Feline Follies.* Metamorphosis, for example, occurs in the very first scene: Master Tom, who is Felix's prototype, hears a female "meow" and his tail detaches to form a question mark, succinctly expressing his curiosity.

Later, as Tom spruces up for a date with "Miss Kitty White," his tail substitutes for a toothbrush. To take a joyride, Tom and Miss Kitty use their tails as the baseboards for two scooters, the wheels of which have formed from four musical notes that sprang from Tom's banjo. Even a color transformation occurs in a scene in which a black mouse drinks a bottle of white milk and gradually assumes the hue of the liquid.

Master Tom's nature is also plastic, continually alternating through-

Opposite: Film frames from *Feline Follies* (1919), the first appearance of the cat who would become Felix. Courtesy Ronald Schwarz.

out the film between animal and human behavior. He first appears as a normal cat standing on all fours, but soon becomes an anthropomorphic "supercat"; not only can he, at will, change his prehensile tail into both functional objects and symbols of the human thought process, but he is also able to stand upright to woo his ladylove, acting and looking like a little man in a cat suit. He can choose to be as magical as the Cheshire Cat or as mundane as an alley tom.

Master Tom is a loner, motivated by life's basics—food, shelter, and sex. He belongs to no man and resembles "The Cat that Walked by Himself," from Rudyard Kipling's 1902 *Just So* story. Unlike the dog companion to Hurd's Bobby Bumps, or Scat the Cat, the pet of Moser's human characters Bud and Susie, Messmer and Sullivan's cat is, from the beginning, an animal *star*, not a supporting player.

Several scenes in *Feline Follies* showcase Messmer's talent for Chaplinesque pantomime. Particularly amusing is Tom's preparation for a date, a "toilette" performed (as the title card says) "with all the care and skill of a debutante." The circular ritualistic victory dance of the mindlessly destructive mice is quite funny, as is Miss Kitty's dance of desire, a hot combination of the shimmy, cancan, balletic elevations, and carnival hootchy-kootch.

There is also a scene of silhouetted people in the windows of white buildings gyrating in extreme distress over Felix's serenade to his lover. ("Scat!" "Vamoose!" "Beat it!" "Stop that noise!" read the square dialogue balloons.) This image predicts Messmer's work twenty years in the future when he would begin a long tenure creating crisp, eloquent silhouette animation for Douglas Leigh's giant electric signs in Times Square.

The cute romantic bubble built throughout the film is cynically burst at the end: Tom is thrown out of his home for dereliction of duty as a mouser, and when he seeks solace from Miss Kitty, she reveals herself to be the mother of a large pack of black kittens; independent, self-centered Tom runs like hell away from her and her brood. We laugh at the violent actions and reactions of the characters to these situations, but our laughter is also an acknowledgment of the filmmaker's contention that the world is an unstable place.

In the final scene, the now homeless, loveless Tom passes a "gas

works" and attempts suicide by putting a gas pump in his mouth and lying down to die. Killing off the hero indicates how one-shot and dead-end a film Messmer and Sullivan thought *Feline Follies* would be, and how unexpected was Famous Players–Lasky's request for a series.

But the shocking finale is also a barometer of the country's mood as America entered the twenties. "The Jazz Age," says historian Geoffrey Perrett, "could with equal justice be termed the Age of Dismay, which may be why it partied so vigorously." A certain alienation and pessimism pervaded the arts, stemming from the "general conviction that another war, even bloodier than the last, was inevitable." Otto Messmer went to war and was one of two million young men exposed to death on a grand scale; that sobering experience is reflected in his unsentimental animation.

The August 2, 1919, *Moving Picture World* announced: "Several strong series of popular animated cartoons will be features of the Paramount Magazine, according to the production plans of Nathan H. Friend, head of the educational department of the Famous Players–

Lasky Corporation. Ten subjects of the Paramount Magazine, which will be issued weekly beginning September 1, already have been completed. The 'Farmer Al Falfa' cartoons by Paul Terry will be seen regularly . . . there will be a new series of animated drawings entitled 'Bud and Susan' by Frank Moser. Pat Sullivan, another well-known cartoonist, also will have a series in which animals will provide an unusual amount of comedy. . . ."

Musical Mews was the title of the second Sullivan-Messmer film, again featuring the mutable black cat. By the third film, his name was changed to Felix, which Messmer said was coined by "Mr. King of Paramount Magazine . . . he suggested the name of Felix, which we kicked around a little bit and decided this was it. Meaning feline and felicity: good-luck cat. So that gave us a theme for [some of] the following [films], to always have him bring good luck to people in trouble."

Felix was not the first film cat. From 1915 to 1918, an animated version of George Herriman's Krazy Kat was produced by Hearst's International Film Service studio. The film series bore little resemblance to Herriman's brilliantly quirky comic strip—the mind-blowing mesas of a surreal Southwest were not used and Krazy's androgynous quality became definitely female.

Felix attracted the public's attention with amazing speed. On March 20, 1920, *Moving Picture World* reported: "Pat Sullivan, creator of Felix the Cat and other animated comics, has signed a long-term contract with the Famous Players–Lasky Corporation to make cartoons for the Paramount Magazine. Outside of Bobby Bumps, Sullivan's cat, Felix, is among the best known character [sic] of the motion picture comics and its antics have a record run at the leading houses throughout the country." "It seems as though the cat's personality was understood and appreciated almost overnight," observes animation historian Donald Crafton. In the December 18, 1920, issue of *Moving Picture World*, a film reviewer noted: "Pat Sullivan put Felix the Cat through some astonishing aquatic and marine adventures with fishes and sailors and ships from which 'Felix' emerges with his usual 'savoir faire.' "

The two-year contract with the Famous Players–Lasky Corporation required Sullivan to deliver one Felix cartoon a month. Messmer now needed help to push out animation footage and in early 1920 Hal

Walker was hired. "Otto was the brains of Felix the Cat," said Walker, "and I was his assistant."

Six years before, Walker was a child actor playing bit parts as "the tough and mischievous kid" in "Heine and Louis" comedies filmed at the Harry Mententhal Studios in Yonkers, New York. "Every direction was extreme pantomime," recalled Walker. "This early training stood me in good stead later with animation." After graduating high school in 1919, Walker "had a hankering for cartooning and so with some nerve and samples I went forth to the big city, New York, to find work."

At the *New York Telegram*, comic-strip cartoonist Milt Gross suggested Walker look up Raoul Barre's studio in the Bronx, where Gross had worked briefly making "jumping pictures."

As he did for so many others, Barre gave young Walker his start in animation. An impressive number of men who went on to become well-known animators and directors passed through Barre's studio, including Pat Sullivan and Gregory La Cava (who gained fame as a live-action director), plus several who found a niche at Walt Disney's studio during its "Golden Era" in the late 1920s and 1930s: Bill Tytla, George Stallings, Burton Gillett, Ben Sharpsteen, Dick Huemer, I. Klein, among others.

Walker went to work at the Sullivan studios in 1920 (perhaps on advice from Barre, Sullivan's former employer), which had moved from Forty-second Street to Sixty-sixth Street and Broadway on Manhattan's Upper West Side. Located on the site where the Juilliard School of Music stands today, the Lincoln Arcade Building was affectionately called by some the Dog Kennel. "With its bowling alley and theatre," writes Peter Salwen, "grimy offices, jewelers' and millinery shops downstairs, its echoing upper floors filled with everything from lawyers and detective agencies to artists and dance students, it was an uptown Bohemia unto itself."

The Sullivan studio, in a poorly lighted small room on the fourth floor, consisted of Pat Sullivan, his wife Marjorie, and Otto Messmer. Walker was hired as Messmer's assistant at "a flat salary of $25 a week."

Walker worked closely with Messmer for nearly a decade and remembers him as a soft-spoken "leader, not a boss. He was my hero.

And always so defensive of Pat, the alcoholic." Sullivan, observed Walker, "was usually ossified," although it was not always apparent. "You wouldn't notice he was drunk, it was a quiet thing. He was a mixed character in his moods. At times, he was exceptionally friendly. Othertimes, he was a bore, a drunken ass." One of Walker's unofficial duties was "trying to escort Pat from the saloon down in the lobby. He needed help, so I'd bring Pat upstairs and put him on a couch. . . . This happened often."

Messmer, who always refused to discuss Sullivan's rape conviction and imprisonment, and whose strongest derogatory remark about his boss was that he was "a weak man," spoke only once in any detail about Sullivan's chronic alcoholism. In that interview, he acknowledged that Sullivan "was a slave to that liquor. He was so continuous [in his drinking] . . . he would take me to the theater once in a while with his wife. I said no a thousand times. But even with that play going on he couldn't sit there without a bottle under the seat. . . . Ushers would carry him out. . . . Shoulda been in a hospital." Messmer defended his

In *Movie Weekly* (December 31, 1921), Pat Sullivan demonstrates how to make cartoons move, with a bear cub and an unnamed Felix-like cat.

Here are two cats ready to be animated. Off hand, they look alike. But peer close—The second one is different. The mouth is open a little more; the whiskers are cocked at a higher angle; the eye is closed a little more. Thus painstakingly are animated cartoons made. Read the article for more details.

boss because he witnessed the man's struggle: "I saw him cry like a baby trying to overcome that weakness. That's why there's sympathy for him. He went to the cardinal there at St. Patrick's [Cathedral]. Tried to get some strength. He couldn't stop that drinking. Terrible."

The general public never knew of Sullivan's problems, nor exactly how the Felix films were made or who actually made them. (Nor did the public care.) Sullivan's name, and only his name, was on the films as producer, so it was clean, convenient, and efficient for the myth-makers of Famous Players–Lasky Corporation's publicity department to reinforce the connection between Pat Sullivan and Felix the Cat. On March 20, 1920, within a few months of Felix's debut, *Moving Picture World* did a puff piece ("Some Short and Snappy Stuff Secured from Sundry Sources") which breathlessly informed readers: "Pat Sullivan, creator of Felix the Cat . . . hails from Sydney, Australia, but he left the antipodes before attaining full majority to continue his art studies in Paris and London. Subsequently, he came to American [*sic*] where he drew cartoons for leading publications, notably the McClure Syndicate and the *Evening World*, gaining added laurels to the name he had acquired through his drawings for leading Australian, English and American publications."

But the attention that Felix was beginning to bring Sullivan threatened to be short-lived when Famous Players–Lasky president Adolph Zukor decided to close down the *Paramount Screen Magazine* as being too costly. Sullivan apparently panicked when he realized that the copyright to Felix belonged, not to him, but to Famous Players–Lasky.

How he retained the rights to Felix is a story that, according to Hal Walker, Sullivan told "once and only once." It seems the distraught cartoonist went to Zukor's office in a drunken "stupor" and urinated on the desk of the president of Famous Players–Lasky, said Walker. In disgust, Zukor asked Sullivan what he wanted.

Zukor took the bread and butter out of his mouth, cried Sullivan, who demanded the copyright to Felix. To avert any further unorthodox negotiations, Zukor quickly phoned the company attorney and told him to honor Sullivan's request.

Sometime in 1921, Sullivan tried to sell a *Felix* series to Warner Brothers, which in 1917 had bought the New York and New Jersey

59

state distribution rights to Barre-Bowers's *Mutt and Jeff* series and in 1921 began distributing Max Fleischer's *Out of the Inkwell* series. Sullivan strolled into the office of Harry Warner's executive secretary, Margaret Winkler, and showed her Felix film samples. She became interested, but H. M. Warner, her boss, did not. However, he encouraged Miss Winkler to take on the distribution of the cartoon series.

During Winkler's seven-year tenure as Warner's secretary, she had gained his respect and confidence, and he felt she had the toughness and business acumen necessary to succeed on her own. Throughout her subsequent career, Margaret "always had counsel from H. M. Warner," according to her brother, George Winkler. To embolden her, Warner offered her the Fleischer *Out of the Inkwell* series when the contract ran out the next year.

Twenty-seven-year-old Margaret Winkler became the first woman producer and distributor of animated films when she and Pat Sullivan signed an agreement on December 15, 1921, for the production and distribution of Felix the Cat cartoons. Winkler's energy, intelligence, and keen business sense would soon open the door to fame and fortune for Sullivan and his cat. (In the fall of 1922, she started distributing the second series of thirteen *Inkwell* cartoons.)

Margaret J. Winkler, about 1921. Courtesy Donald Crafton.

The "J" in her name had no meaning; she just liked the way "M. J. Winkler" sounded. She also felt that until she gained a secure foothold in the male-dominated film field, it would be wise to let businessmen assume they were dealing with a man.

In February 1922, Winkler announced in trade journals that she "has severed her connections with the Warners, with whom she has been actively identified for a number of years, and will branch out in the independent field with her own company. . . . Her plans embrace the formation of a large distributing unit with headquarters in New York and production offices in Los Angeles. . . ." She also let it be known that the "series of animated cartoon comics, known as 'Felix' which are animated by the Pat Sullivan Studios and which for two years were distributed and exploited by Paramount was acquired last week [*sic*] by Miss Winkler for independent distribution." There is also an indication that Winkler demanded from Sullivan a better-quality Felix film than before, and would make him toe the mark; in the February 23, 1922, *Ex-*

Mr. State Rights Buyer—Listen!

Pat Sullivan, my boss, has just made a contract with Miss Winkler to star me in a series of twelve cartoon comics. I am the only trained cat in the movies—and oh boy, can I act. For information about my new distributing arrangement, drop a line to

M. J. WINKLER
220 W. 42nd St.   New York

hibitor's Trade Review, Winkler's release said: "It is expected with extensive improvements in story, photography and animation the new series will gain favor with even more persons than before."

There is reason to believe that Sullivan produced a couple of Felix films on his own between the dissolution of the Famous Players–Lasky contract and signing an agreement with Winkler. The Winkler contract specifically acknowledges that "producer [Sullivan] has produced two [Felix animated] cartoons, which have been inspected by the Distributor [Winkler] and are agreed upon by the parties hereto as being acceptable and accepted by the Distributor, and the Producer [Sullivan] agrees to produce ten additional Felix Animated Cartoons each of which shall be . . . approximately 600 to 800 foot in length" commencing December 22, 1921.

Also, in handwritten notes for a film chronology prepared for a 1976 Felix the Cat film retrospective in Canada, Otto Messmer wrote: "When the [Screen] Magazine ceased . . . I made a pilot [film] *Felix Saves the Day*." It is probable that, despite Felix's initial popularity, potential distributors such as Winkler were not pleased with the format or the quality of the films. Sullivan needed to prove he could produce Felix films independently of the *Paramount Screen Magazine* that could match those of the competition.

Felix Saves the Day has a screen time of seven minutes and twenty seconds, almost double *Feline Follies*' length, and there is evidence

61

within *Felix Saves the Day* to indicate Sullivan was attempting to compete on a par with the cartoon series of his peers. The opening title copies Fleischer's *Out of the Inkwell* premise in which the main character (Koko the Clown) is introduced by the hand of the animating artist. (Messmer's 1916 short, *Trials of a Movie Cartoonist*, explored this self-reflexive motif.) Here, a hand holds a pen from which Felix emerges tailless. As blobs of black ink continue to squeeze out of the pen and form the name "Felix," the angular cat attempts to catch them and stick them to his rump. Finally, he succeeds and is a whole cat, as the title also becomes complete by announcing, "Felix—a Pat Sullivan Cartoon." Nowhere in the title is Paramount or Winkler mentioned, a further indication that the film was independently made.

Saves the Day intercuts still photographs and live-action footage between several animation scenes. Sullivan may have been attempting to economize on a personally financed project by limiting the amount of animation while still providing the extra footage needed to make a complete reel. To Messmer, who had to photograph the stills, register the animation to them, and hire a free-lance cinematographer to shoot the crowd at one of Babe Ruth's baseball games, the technique was "a nuisance" and "too much work."

The film, however, is a delightful early showcase of the unexpected visual absurdities that audiences would come to expect in a Felix film. Felix uses his tail when pitching a practice baseball game with street urchins. One of the boys, Willie Brown, bats the ball into a cop's mouth and is chased up the side of a photo of Manhattan's Metropolitan Tower building. A special "fly cop" soars over the cityscape to arrest Willie and imprison him in the Tombs, the drawing of which is based on a photograph Messmer took of the city prison. (Willie's predicament recalls Sullivan's unhappy experience in the Tombs, now turned into a private joke. Sullivan's former comic strip is alluded to when the opposing baseball team—the "Tar Heels"—are seen as a group of *Sammy Johnsin* clones.)

Felix paces back and forth, hands behind his back, racking his cartoon brain to figure out a solution to the problem, an early example of one of his most memorable trademark mannerisms. Like a vaudeville trouper, Felix communicates directly with the audience. He winks at us, takes us into his confidence, and anticipates his actions in broad pantomime gestures. In this case, his questioning manifests itself in a string of question marks that spring from his head and sit one on top of the other, as tall as the prison building; Felix uses the question marks as a ladder to visit Willie.

Square-shaped balloons and full-screen title cards—holdovers from comic strips—contain more continuity information than is needed; as Messmer and his animators gained confidence over the years in their mime acting abilities, use of balloons and dialogue cards was minimized. Felix arrives at Yankee Stadium to take Willie's place in the game after live-action intercuts of a taxicab and an elevated train. Several live-action shots show straw-hatted men rising in the bleachers and sitting as if in reaction to the cartoon action on the field. Animation never appears in the same frame as the live-action, but their relationship is implied by crosscutting between the two techniques.

Willie's team is losing, so Felix proves himself to be a good-luck cat by knocking a high fly into the heavens, hitting Jupiter Pluvius sitting on a cloud. In revenge, the Roman sky god makes the rain fall on the players so the game has to be called. Felix reverts to his cat nature by running on all fours back to Willie in prison to tell him the news. Both perform a merry dance Felix will often use to express extreme joy: placing a finger atop his head and turning, as if a maypole, while kicking his legs in a giddy jig.

Winkler agreed to pay Sullivan $1,000 each for the first six Felix films, $1,200 for the second six, and 50 percent of all moneys from the foreign sales of all twelve shorts. The contract between them was negotiated for Sullivan by Harry Kopp.

Nineteen twenty-one would prove to be the real beginning of Pat Sullivan's rise to international fame and fortune through Felix the Cat; as an architect of that rise, Harry Kopp would share monetarily in Sullivan's luck. However, Margaret Winkler, another architect of the joint career of Felix the Cat and Pat Sullivan, would not fare as well. She would not endure like Kopp; in fact, her services would in due course be terminated after she had served her purpose as "the great live-wire saleslady."

But not without a fight.

THE WINKLER YEARS, 1921–1925

MARGARET WINKLER wasted no time. By early March 1922, the dynamic distributor sold the entire series of twelve Felix cartoons to Elk Photoplays for northern New Jersey and New York City.

By mid-March, Winkler closed the California, Iowa, and Nebraska rights to the series. By the end of the month, she boasted in *Moving Picture World* (March 25, 1922) that the Felix series "has been contracted for and shown in such theatres as Grauman's million dollar theatre in Los Angeles, the imposing Des Moines Theatre in Des Moines, the discriminating Rivoli Theatre in New York, the chain of Finklestein and Ruben Theatres in Minneapolis and St. Paul, the Marcus Loew theatres in New York, the Abe Blank circuit of theatres in Nebraska and other representative motion picture playhouses in all sections of the country." By April 1, Winkler reported that 60 percent of the country had been sold her Felix cartoon, including Canada.

In addition to booking the films, Winkler was also papering the trade journals with a blizzard of press releases and advertisements touting the new series and its star. The promotional blitz and Felix's individuality created an immediate impact. In his review of *Saves the Day*, the first of the series released (on February 1), Matthew A. Taylor of the February 11, 1922, *Motion Picture News* praised Felix as "a delightful cartoon character. He is given a distinct personality." The March 11 *Film Daily* noted that the "animation is clever and will provoke a good deal of laughter."

Each new release was aggressively promoted by Winkler; *Felix at*

Opposite: A wood-jointed, leather-eared Felix toy from the 1920s, manufactured by Schoenhut.

the Fair, the second of the series (released March 1, 1922), "is said to contain as many laughs as there are feet in the film," according to the publicity placement in the March 11 issue of *Moving Picture World*. *Motion Picture News* of April 8 breathlessly announced the arrival of the third Felix film (released April 1): "Pat Sullivan completed last week the work of editing, titling and assembling his latest subject, and a sample print of FELIX MAKES GOOD was rushed to the offices of Miss Winkler for private review."

Winkler's publicity sometimes neglected to mention Sullivan, and worse, as in the April 1 *Moving Picture World* announcement, she called Felix "her" cartoon series. Surely, this did not sit well with the man who went to extreme lengths to retrieve his "bread and butter" from Adolph Zukor, and who would hold a proprietary paranoia regarding Felix's ownership throughout his career. This tension and others between Sullivan and Winkler regarding artistic control were publicly addressed on April 8 in *Motion Picture News* in a conciliatory statement aimed at calming Sullivan:

> Pat Sullivan, celebrated cartoonist and creator of the "Felix" cartoon comics, the series of which are controlled for world-wide distribution by Miss M. J. Winkler, will henceforth be responsible for the poster illustrations as well as the subject matter of "Felix" comics.

By May, Felix had become so popular around the country, his image was placed on a "stuffed toy form" in three sizes of black and white velvet produced by the Gund Company, "Manufacturers of High Quality Animals and Novelties." In a trade advertisement, Pat Sullivan is listed prominently as "Artist-Originator" of "Felix the Movie Cat," and Felix is shown playing a banjo, smoking a pipe, and, in five sequential drawings, becoming drunk from a found jug of booze. Obviously, Felix's appeal was aimed toward adults rather than children. A "News Note" on Gund's advertisement in the May issue of *Playthings* magazine confirms it, explaining that a test marketing gimmick started the "toy craze for Felix . . . in Atlantic City, N.J., when scores of bathing beauties and boardwalk strollers carried the little cats along the ocean front." This initial foray into merchandising Felix provided easy additional

income for Sullivan and encouraged him to exploit his cat's image on innumerable products.

A number of cartoon characters were marketed as toys before Felix came on the scene, including Little Nemo and the gang from Slumberland, the Yellow Kid, Happy Hooligan, Krazy Kat, Mutt and Jeff, and the Katzenjammer Kids, among others. But the fame and popularity of such characters stemmed from comic strips rather than animated films. With Felix, it was the other way around: he was the first character created specifically for animation whose image was exploited as a doll or toy (and later in a comic strip). And until Mickey Mouse came along, no cartoon character was exploited more widely or successfully.

At the Sullivan studio, Messmer, Walker, and a few blackeners turned out one film each month that further defined the Felix persona and solidified his relationship with moviegoers. The vague titles do not

Two advertisements from *The Exhibitor*, a trade journal, (left) September 15 and (right) October 15, 1922. Courtesy Robert and Katherine Fish.

indicate the imaginative breadth of the stories and the humorous details packed into each one, e.g., *Felix All at Sea* (released May 1, 1922), *Felix in the Swim* (July 1), *Felix Finds a Way* (August 1), *Felix Gets Revenge* (September 1), *Felix on the Trail* (November 1), *Felix Gets Left* (December 1), and so on.

Felix in Love (June 1), for example, combines elements of the *Arabian Nights* and Kipling's *Just So Stories*, taking us via a magical genie in a lamp from Felix's generic American backyard to an African jungle. Felix's adventure begins when one of his basic needs—this time, sex—is frustrated by his girlfriend's refusal to succumb to his singing. "I bet," Felix's dialogue balloon tells us, "if I was in Africa, she'd miss me." Inspired by glancing through a book about Aladdin, Felix rubs a throwaway lamp and a goofy-looking slave appears to grant his wish to travel. Immediately, the drawn lines of his hometown dissolve and transform into a palm-tree setting. In this cartoon version of Africa, a log becomes a crocodile and a tin lizzie turns into a hippo. Felix battles for his life, but his struggle for survival exudes a Chaplin-like insouciance. Escaping hostile monkeys, Felix pays silent homage to his spiritual father by affecting the Little Tramp's famous one-legged turn around a corner.

The Felix films made during the first year of the Winkler contract do not use metamorphosis as audaciously or irrationally as future ones would. Felix alternates between behaving like a four-legged cat and a two-legged man; in *Felix Minds the Kid* (October 1), for example, his tail is prehensile as it bounces a ball, but it does not detach to actually become objects. For his final escape, Felix makes a striped peppermint stick unfold into an umbrella, but in future films (such as *Romeeow* in 1927) the umbrella would most often form from his tail. The kid in *Minds the Kid* is also rationally changed; his shape becomes that of an airship when he inhales the air from a balloon. In *Felix Turns the Tide* (October 15, 1922), Felix boosts himself into a cannon in front of a cannonball before being shot into enemy lines, instead of becoming a cannonball himself.

What these early films did do was bond Felix to the moviegoing public by thoroughly familiarizing them with his personality and mannerisms. He constantly checks in with the audience, looking out from the screen to wink conspiratorially before a caper (or during one), and he anticipates his actions by holding up a finger, as if to say, "Watch this." Viewers came to know and expect certain others of his pantomimic gestures and actions: Felix thrusting his clenched fists straight down in front of him and shaking them when frustrated and angry; his giddy jigs and maypole twirlings when in love or extremely happy; the "eureka!" gesture of one hand swung from the side to the front of his chest when an idea burst forth from his cartoon brain; and his most celebrated mannerism, the hunched-over pacing hands-behind-back while in deep thought.

It is important to remember that Felix was a thinking character, not a mindless action figure like cartoons from other studios of the period. He contemplated problems and found solutions appropriate to the medium of animation, where the impossible reigns supreme. Because of the time required for Felix to think about his predicament and come up with an idea before executing it, the pacing of the films is slower, or rather more stop-and-go, than it might otherwise have been. In the early films, the development of Felix's pantomimic human gestures and facial expressions, and his calculated approach to problems, endeared him to audiences and prepared them for the increasingly bizarre metamorphic effects in the films that followed.

As a showcase of Felix's "acting" abilities, *Felix Turns the Tide* is one of the finest of the Winkler series. It is a war story, and the authenticity of the emotions portrayed by Felix undoubtedly came directly from Otto Messmer, who transformed the memory of his hellish wartime experiences into art.

The film does not dive into action scenes at the front lines until it has carefully established sympathy for Felix and his predicament. Rats have declared war on cats and Felix (puffing up his furry chest with manly pride) decides patriotically to join the fray. But first, there is a heartfelt good-bye from a sad-faced Felix to his human friend, a butcher shop owner, who tells Felix to "call me anytime you need help" (thus setting up the film's zany ending). Felix next says farewell to his girlfriend, a white cat, who, after Felix proposes on bended knee, promises to marry him when he returns. The two cats tenderly embrace and kiss, while two heart symbols of their love merge above them. There are no jokes in these opening scenes, except for one brief funny glimpse of a continuous swarm of cats piling helter-skelter into a recruitment tent and emerging, cookie-cutter-like, as marching, gun-toting soldiers.

Felix soon enters that same recruitment tent and comes out the other side brandishing a bayonet with appropriate killer gestures Messmer no doubt recalled from his own basic training. Immediately, the scene shifts to a raging battle seen from an overhead cosmic view. Tiny figures advancing in authentic-looking formations toward a ridge are rebuffed violently. To simulate bomb explosions, Messmer alternates the colors black and white in every other frame for landscapes, objects, and characters, creating a disorienting flicker. He also poured white salt onto a black card under the animation camera and traced designs in the salt with his fingers frame by frame for smoke and explosion effects.

The authenticity of the visuals as remembered truths is reinforced when a bomb knocks a dozen cats over a rise and they land motionless on the ground. There are also two cuts to completely still drawings of the bodies of dead cats strewn on the battlefield. Felix registers convincing facial and body expressions of horror and a determination to conquer the enemy forces. This is accomplished in a marvelously funny way: Felix calls his butcher friend, who sends, through telephone wires, a platoon of hot dogs. The sight of Felix leading a battle charge on an enemy fortress followed by hundreds of wiener warriors ranks as one of cinema's great Absurdist images. (After the grim intensity of the earlier battle scenes, we laugh as much from relief as from the sight of the sausage soldiers.)

Felix receives a medal for heroism and joyfully marches at the head of a homecoming parade. His butcher friend hugs and kisses him, one of the very few times Felix ever allowed a human such intimacies (but emotions run high at wartime victory celebrations). Typically, the film ends on a refreshingly cynical note: Felix's girl was not faithful to him, but married another. She is glimpsed yelling at and slapping her beleaguered husband as they lead a seemingly endless line of kittens. Laughing at what he calls a "narrow escape," Felix equates marriage with war.

The film series continued to snowball through 1922, attracting more bookings and excellent reviews. P. W. Gallico of the *New York Daily*

News (who later gained fame as sportswriter and novelist Paul Gallico) reviewed *Felix Wakes Up* (released on September 15) on November 10 and liked best "the delightful elasticity of Mr. Sullivan's elephant. . . . The elephant which Felix encounters in his endeavors to recapture an escaped zoo lion is not the least hidebound. In fact, he makes his first appearance out of a knothole in a tree. This was a soul-satisfying moment to us." As for Felix, Gallico found him "the feline spirit incarnate, the Eva Tanguay of Tabbies. We're for five reels of Felix and only one reel of other folks."

Although three months remained on their old contract, Margaret Winkler wrote a letter to Pat Sullivan on September 12, 1922, supplementing the agreement between them regarding a second series of Felix cartoons. Due to the success of the first series and the demand for more product, the next output of films was to be doubled to twenty-four subjects delivered at the rate of one every two weeks.

The previous contract stated it was to be automatically renewed at a price of $3 per negative foot. Thus, if the films ran 800 feet, Winkler would have been obligated to pay Sullivan $2,400 per film. Instead, the new agreement asked for films not less than 650 feet, and agreed to pay Sullivan $1,750 per short, an increase of only $550 per film from the previous year. But doubling the annual number of films would increase Sullivan's total compensation by $29,800.

"It is further understood and agreed," wrote Winkler, "that I shall have the first option on a further series of these comics at the same price." This almost casually written sentence would eventually be hotly challenged in the courts and cause Winkler to lose lucrative Felix.

With Sullivan secured for another year, Winkler proceeded to

Part of an advertisement for Felix dolls by Gund, in the May 1922 *Playthings* magazine.

arrange for international distribution of Felix through Pathé Film in London.

Sullivan's increased productivity in the coming year necessitated an increase in staff and a larger working space. The studio moved in 1923 for a third and final time across Broadway from the Lincoln Arcade to a well-lit second-floor loft at 47 West Sixty-third Street.

In 1922, Sullivan allowed Messmer to hire Bill Nolan as the first of a number of, as Messmer called them, "guest animators." Twenty-eight-year-old Nolan, once the foreman of Barre's staff when Sullivan worked there, was considered by his peers to be one of the fastest animators who ever lived, able, if necessary, to push out seven hundred drawings a day. Nolan's forte was action scenes, which he drew "straight ahead," the term for the dominant animation method of the day.

Straight-ahead animation is drawn from position A to position Z, one drawing after the other. Winsor McCay used a "split" method in which he divided an action into sections—extreme poses—which were filled in with "in-between" drawings. In this way, McCay knew where his action was going and could control it, which is why his animation is so well timed and contains such strong storytelling/acting poses. Straight-ahead animation is fine for eccentric, funny action, but the control possible with the "extreme/in-between" method made it the system of choice when sound came to animation in the late 1920s.

Bill Nolan has also been described as a man who was relentless in his "search for ways to make life easier for himself." This led him to devise certain "tricks" that helped to decrease the labor-intensiveness of animation and were eventually absorbed into the industry at large. At the Barre studio, for instance, Nolan is said to have been the first animator to use a panorama ("pan") background, a background whose width is two or three times the size of the cels containing the character drawings. By sliding a long pan background frame by frame under a series of cels that repeat—"cycle"—a character walking or running, the number of cels necessary for the action is reduced.

When William Randolph Hearst hired Nolan to work at the short-lived International Film Service (IFS) animation studio (1915–1918), the animator developed what became known throughout the industry as "rubber-hose" animation. Instead of bending a cartoon character's

arms, wrists, and knees at the joints (a series of successive breaks, as in nature), Nolan eliminated the angularity (and realism) of that action by substituting smooth hoselike connections for the limbs. Arms and legs that resembled macaroni looked and moved funny, and were easy to draw and animate. It was perfect for zany animated action, a surefire guarantee of laughs from the audience. Walter Lantz, who worked with Nolan at IFS, affirms Nolan "created a new style, and it loosened up animation."

Nolan stayed only two years at the Sullivan studio (leaving in late 1924), but his need to simplify character designs in order to facilitate animating brought a major change to Felix the Cat. "When I first learned to draw the cat," recalled Hal Walker, "he looked like a fox and he was angular in every respect. It was the influence of the famous silhouette artist Tony Sarg. He impressed Otto, that if you want to have anything black, it must be sharp and angular, shouldn't be curved." Because Bill Nolan had a difficult time drawing the snout on Felix, he eliminated it. "The circular round [Felix] was Bill Nolan's creation," said Hal Walker. "The original Felix was Otto's, [but] Nolan made the cat round all over." Donald Crafton explains that "the rounded shape made Felix seem more cuddly and sympathetic, and

Two film frames from *Felix Revolts* (1923). Courtesy Donald Crafton.

circles were faster to draw, retrace, ink and blacken." Nolan struggled with the foxy-boxy-looking Felix for a year, but by 1924 the cat's now familiar circular design was firmly in place, with Messmer's blessing.

Nineteen twenty-three saw the angular Felix involved with union organizing (*Felix Revolts*, released May 1), when humans begin to "treat us cats like dogs" by starving the "feline pests out of our town." Felix leads his fellow pussies in a sit-down strike of their duties as mousers, until the mayor and townsfolk beg the cats to return and rid the town of rats. Felix raises his left arm in a power gesture at film's end, but his motivation throughout is not based on political ideology, but rather (and as usual) on his self-preservationist instincts.

A significant element in the popularity of Felix films was the way they mirrored trends in American lifestyles in the 1920s. *Felix Strikes It Rich* (July 1) presents Felix as a quintessential "jazz baby," blowing a hot saxophone that causes the neighborhood chickens to forgo egg laying for uninhibited dancing. (The film is a good example of the way Messmer's staccato acting animation of Felix blended deftly with Nolan's funny, rubbery action animation of the chickens.)

By 1923, King Oliver's Creole Jazz Band's trail-blazing influence resulted in jazz bands flourishing across the country, and in the next year Paul Whiteman would bring his whitewashed "up-tempo parody of what he imagined black music would sound like" to Carnegie Hall. It is a small irony to see Felix, whose design was adapted from a black character, playing with gusto music created by black Americans. Yet Felix, his animation full of unexpected changes, improvisational developments, and metamorphic riffs, is the essence of jazz.

Young moderns of the twenties loved to dance, everything from the foxtrot to the camel walk, shuffle, and tango. In 1924, the Charleston arrived, a wild, arms-flailing new dance craze. Felix sometimes imitated the Charleston (in his films as well as in still publicity drawings). His movie pantomime performances are dancelike in the way he expresses abandon, joy, and senselessness. His movements are the opposite of the lyricism and gracefulness of the waltz, the dance of an older generation, which the Charleston dancers rejected in favor of speed, frenetic energy, and abandon.

Dissembling and reassembling his form, Felix is a Cubist cat, a symbol of postwar modernism. Far removed from the prewar artnouveau-ish curvilinear and fluid animation of Winsor McCay, Felix (especially before Bill Nolan redesigned him) is full of angles that fragment and juxtapose in exciting new ways.

Besides music and dancing, *Felix Strikes It Rich* also contains an allusion to the "new woman," so different from her prewar counterpart. The sexist male animators mock the "Flappers," who smoked cigarettes, wore short skirts and bobbed their hair, were sexually active, and held down jobs outside the home. A rooster in *Strikes It Rich* chastises a dance-mad, pleasure-seeking hen for, as the dialogue balloon says, "getting too sophisticated."

Racial, sexual, and ethnic stereotypes abound in the Felix films, reflecting American attitudes of the time. Females are either passive, fickle teases, e.g., *Felix in Love* (1922), *Comicalamities* (1928), or rolling-pin-toting harridan wives, e.g., *Woos Whoopee* (1930 or 1928), *Whys and Otherwhys* (1927). Blacks are easily frightened or duped, e.g., the hat-buying mammy and the black man who loses his pants in *Felix Goes Hungry* (1924), and, designed according to the Sammy Johnsin model, their white-masked black heads resembling Felix; often blacks are depicted as ferocious cannibals. Jews are only shown working in pawnshops, e.g., *Felix Goes Hungry*, or tailor shops, e.g., *Felix Trifles with Time* (1925). Homophobia surfaces in *Felix in Fairyland* (1923): when a housefly claims to be a fairy, Felix bursts into a swish dance

I'LL HAVE TO SACRIFICE MY ART AND GO IN THE MOVIES,

across the room until the fly corrects him, "No. I'm a *real* fairy." In *Felix in Love*, the hippo, metamorphosed from a tin lizzie, mistakes the auto's nickname for a slang word for lesbian and angrily asks, "Who are you calling a lizzie?"

The Felix the Cat films were clearly intended for an adult audience. In *Felix Dopes It Out* (1924), an alcoholic tramp (whose bulbous nose is so hot it can light a cigarette) learns from Felix the cure for a red nose: "Keep on drinking and it'll turn blue." Felix holds a casual approach to death, which is understandable, since he manages to survive all disasters. Still, his world is often one of unblinking cruelty, violence, and (sometimes) wholesale slaughter, e.g., the cat corpses in *Felix Turns the Tide* (1922). In *Felix Hunts the Hunter* (1926), the film's death motif is announced in the first scene when a stricken bird falls between Felix and a pith-helmeted human big-game huntsman. Later, an ostrich eats a gun and coughs bullets, shooting an elephant between the eyes, severing the neck of a giraffe, shattering a hippo (whose angel flies heavenward), and collapsing a bear, among other unfortunate creatures. Felix triumphantly hauls the bird and beast carcasses across a jungle landscape, places a foot on a dead lion, and puffs out his chest to proudly claim credit for the inadvertent mass murder.

Felix's personality, his design, and the content of his films communicated with audiences and delighted them as no other film cartoon had before. In *Felix in Hollywood* (July 15, 1923), the cartoon cat meets and mingles with human gods and goddesses of the silent silver screen, a tacit acknowledgment of the public's recognition of Felix's star stature and equality among human movie icons.

The film opens as a shabby and hungry stage actor (of the sort Messmer must have seen countless times in Hoboken theater melodramas) paces his bare room and proclaims, "I'll have to sacrifice my art and go in the movies." Felix sympathetically imitates the actor's walk and gestures until the actor regally orders him, "Go ye forth and procure the wherewithal for sustenance and transportation to Hollywood."

In town, Felix comes upon a customerless shoestore with a sign reading BANKRUPT and a weeping proprietor. Felix ponders an idea, twirling his whiskers like a mustache. "Eureka!" pose. He buys and chews a wad of one-cent gum, which he places all over the streets. Shoes of dozens of unwary passers-by are pulled off, and the gum victims rush (of course) to the shoestore to re-cover their unshod tootsies. Grateful, the shoestore owner gives Felix $500, which solves the actor's travel problem.

In Hollywood at "Static Studios," Felix looks for a job in the movies. He meets Gloria Swanson and Ben Turpin (who teaches Felix how to cross his eyes), and auditions for big-eared Will Hays.

Felix's performance in *Felix In Hollywood* allows him an extended showcase of acting and performing skills seldom attempted by silent-cartoon characters, and is a forerunner of the emphasis on personality development in the Disney sound-cartoon era of the 1930s. For his audition for Will Hays, Felix is always his irrepressible self, commenting on his actions by winking and laughing with us, the audience, as he expresses "sorrow" and "joy." It's all a lark to him, and for a finale, he offers "something original." Detaching his tail and using it as a cane, acquiring a mustache and stretching out his square feet, Felix shrugs while breaking into a lopsided gait and becomes Charlie Chaplin.

77

Felix the Cat meets Charlie Chaplin in *Felix in Hollywood* (1923).

He twirls his tail/cane, swings it into the air, catches it, and skids on one foot out of scene. It is a beautiful performance, thanks to Messmer's recall of his analysis of the Little Tramp's actions in the old Chaplin animated film series. He animates Chaplin one final time when Felix bumps into the star, who accuses the cat of "stealing my stuff."

Felix is distracted by the sight of Douglas Fairbanks tied to a post fighting off giant mosquitos. ("Gosh! The Three Muskeeters have got him.") Felix's tail borrows William S. Hart's gun, shoots all the insects but one, who literally stares daggers at Felix. The cartoon cat grabs one to use as a sword and vanquishes the bug. Cecile B. De Mille steps forward to inform Felix that his extraordinary bravery was captured on film; in the final scene, Felix proudly holds "one of those long-term contracts."

Meanwhile, back in the real world, Pat Sullivan and Harry Kopp were also dealing with contracts for Felix in both the film and print media. The producer signed with Hearst's King Features Syndicate for a weekly Sunday color-page comic strip, to be called simply *Felix*. The strip began nationally on Sunday, September 2, 1923, but its first appearance in the United States was on Friday, August 31, in the *Boston American*: for several months, the Boston paper ran the comic supplement (*Your Sunday Treat*) every day in the week to attract readers and test-market new strips.

However, Felix's very first appearance in comic-strip form was in London on August 1, 1923, in *The Sketch*. It is an indication of how popular Felix had become in England due to the Winkler-Pathé European distribution of the films. On August 8, the *Illustrated London News* offered readers a full explanation of "How the Moving Film Drawing is Made [for] . . . the Great Film 'Comedian,' Felix the Cat."

Although the weekly American Felix strip enjoyed a lengthy run until September 19, 1943, the public, according to Mark Johnson, "never completely embraced it." This may have been due to readers perceiving the strip as merely an advertisement for the film series, a fate that befell the short-lived Charlie Chaplin strip distributed by the Keely Syndicate in 1915.

Also, in contrast to the Felix film cartoons, the Felix strip was out of step with the times. The only other "funny animal" strip of conse-

quence in the 1920s was George Herriman's *Krazy Kat* (1913–1944), which would have died from public indifference had not W. R. Hearst himself loved it and personally kept it in print. "People"/"domestic comedy" strips were popular, such as *Polly and Her Pals, Bringing Up Father, Mutt and Jeff*, and *The Katzenjammer Kids*.

There were also a number of "working women" strips that sprang up during the twenties, such as *Somebody's Stenog* by Alfred Hayward, *Winnie Winkle, the Breadwinner* by Martin Brenner, *Tillie the Toiler* by Russ Westover, and *Miss Information* by Wood Cohen. The year following Felix's strip debut, 1924, saw the start of "action" strips, such as *Little Orphan Annie* and *Wash Tubbs*, "people" strips whose strong human characters and suspense/threat-of-death stories captured a war-sobered public's interest. Winsor McCay's 1924–1926 revival of his once-popular fantasy strip, *Little Nemo in Slumberland*, proved to be hopelessly out of touch with the public.

The signature on the Felix comic strip read "Pat Sullivan," but it was Otto Messmer who supplemented his studio salary each week by ghosting both the stories and the drawings for the strip. As a small acknowledgment of how much creative and managerial responsibility Messmer had come to assume for the smooth running of Sullivan's burgeoning enterprises, Sullivan placed Messmer's name opposite his

79

own on the studio's stationery, as if he were a partner in the company. (Messages had to be short and written small in order to fit on Sullivan's stationery; besides the names "Pat Sullivan," "O. Messmer," and the address and phone number of "The Pat Sullivan Studios," the crowded letterhead contained "The Studios with a Reputation"; "Producers of the 'Felix' Cartoons"; "Specialists in Animated Drawings, Comedy Cartoons, Industrial Films, Advertising Films and Technical Drawings, Titles, Trailers"; and finally, "If it's anything in animation, we make them.")

The Felix strip's action was encased in twelve inflexible box panels with a rectangular banner drawing across the top of the page relating to the story below. To save time and creative energy, the extremely busy Messmer often reused ideas, plots, and sometimes actual scenes from the films.

The first Felix strip appearing in the *Boston American* on August 31, for example, borrows a theme—Felix reversing his habits as a mouser in order to forcibly elicit respect from a human—from the film *Felix Revolts*, which was released May 1; in the September 14 *American* strip, the second half of the story copies Felix's discovery of oil after being forced to dig his grave at gunpoint in *Felix Strikes It Rich*, released July 1; the house-wrecking mice from 1919's *Feline Follies* show up in the September 28 strip; and the entire gum-on-the-shoe gag from *Felix in Hollywood* (July 15, 1923) is in the November 2 *American* strip, including some of the dialogue balloons, e.g., "I'm that hungry I could eat the dates off a calendar."

At the time of the comic strip's debut, Sullivan became embroiled in a contract dispute with his film distributor Margaret Winkler and her fiancé, Charles B. Mintz. (They were married November 24, 1923.) On August 29, 1923, a letter signed by Winkler was sent to Sullivan exercising the option contained in her letter of September 12 of the previous year for a further series of twenty-four Felix films at the same length (650 feet) and price ($1,750 per negative), commencing no later than January 1, 1924. The Winkler office was attempting to continue distributing Sullivan's by now extremely popular film series without paying more money for them.

Charles B. Mintz (1889–1939) met Margaret Winkler in 1915 when

COMIC SUPPLEMENT
REGULAR FEATURE
EVERY DAY

BOSTON AMERICAN
LARGEST EVENING CIRCULATION IN NEW ENGLAND

September 14, 1923

YOUR SUNDAY TREAT
EVERY DAY
IN THE WEEK

Felix

he was a booking agent for Warner Brothers at the so-called House of Forty Thieves, a.k.a. the Warner sales office at 146 West Forty-fifth Street. After rising through the ranks to become a Warner executive, Mintz joined Winkler's independent company in 1922. Winkler Productions was a family-run organization with Margaret's brother George as office manager and later West Coast production supervisor, Margaret concentrating on marketing and exploitation, and Charles negotiating deals and contracts. Eventually, Charles became president of Winkler Productions when his wife retired to raise their two children.

Sullivan consulted Harry Kopp regarding Winkler's letter, and the lawyer felt the alleged option, although vaguely worded and ambiguous, was one that Winkler Productions assumed it could hold forever and assert at any time. In an attempt to break the agreement, Sullivan, on Kopp's advice, fired off a reply the next day (August 30) to Winkler, stating, "I do not intend to make any further series of Felix cartoons after the expiration of the present series to consist of 24 subjects of

SQUATING
GEO. CANNATA
AL EUGSTER

STANDING L TO R
AL ZAMORA
JACK BOGLE
T. BURNS
OTTO MESSMER*
DANA PARKER *
ALBERT THUBER *
BURTON GILETTE

BLACK SUIT - HAL WALKER

1925
63 st. STUDIO

Felix the Collectible. Right: ten toys. Collection of Michael Del Castello. Below: Felix with cigar and Minnie Mouse together on a rare Spanish picnic basket, 1930; soft Gund doll, c. 1940; Nifty Co. wind-up scooter, c. 1930. Collection of Felix Cappadona. Three wooden dolls with bendable arms, c. 1920. Collection Samuels Museum of Comic Toys.

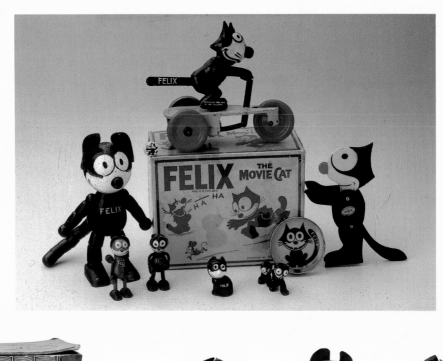

Opposite: Felix chinaware, c. 1920s. Collection of Felix Cappadona. Schoenhut Felix doll. Collection Samuels Museum of Comic Toys. Japanese Felix toy, c. 1930. Collection of Felix Cappadona. Box of Felix dolls, c. 1926. Collection Keith Kaonis/The Inside Collector.

Above: Felix doodles by Otto Messmer, c. 1970. Courtesy Doris Messmer. Right: the three stages of Felix, c. 1922 (left), c. 1926 (center), and c. 1960 (right).

650 ft. in length. The new series, if issued, will consist of more than 24 subjects, and of much greater length than 650 ft."

That fall, Mintz tried to persuade Sullivan a number of times to agree to continue making the films under his and his wife's claimed option, including two meetings in November (one with Margaret Winkler Mintz) at Harry Kopp's office. All attempts at negotiations and agreements for a price in excess of $1,750 failed.

"Pat Sullivan," said George Winkler, "was a small man with a fiery temper. He wanted more for his product, but he boosted his price way too high."

So Sullivan entered into a contract with distributor Joe Brandt for the sale of twenty-six Felix films of not less than 700 feet for the sum of $3,500 each, which was double the Mintz offer.

When Mr. and Mrs. Mintz heard of the new contract, they quickly took an ad in the trade newspaper *The Film Daily* on December 19, 1923, which effectively scared Brandt, who canceled his deal with Sullivan. The advertisement, signed Margaret J. Winkler, read:

WARNING.

Definite knowledge has come to me that a series of "FELIX" the Cat Comedy Cartoons by Pat Sullivan, is being offered on the Motion Picture market.

I am handling the 1922 and 1923 series of "FELIX." On September 12, 1922 an option was given me by Pat Sullivan for the next series. I exercised that option on August 29th, 1923.

I intend to protect my rights where "FELIX" is concerned and will use extreme legal measures if necessary to do so.

Sullivan briefly visited Australia to spend Christmas with his now blind father. His distress over losing the lucrative Brandt contract is apparent in a peevish interview in which "Mr. Sullivan declared that he did not intend to draw Australian animals instead of Felix." The Vancouver "shipping reporter" aboard the Sydney-bound ship *Acrangi* described Sullivan as a "white-haired, short, dyspeptic-looking man," and a photograph shows him looking disgruntled, baggy-eyed, and much older than his thirty-eight years.

In early February of the new year, Kopp sought a declaratory court judgment to determine the legality of Winkler's alleged option clause for Sullivan's services and to sort out the rights of both parties. A trial was scheduled for the end of April, but in the meantime Mr. and Mrs. Mintz renewed negotiations with Sullivan and Kopp for an adjustment of their differences and a settlement of the court action started by Sullivan. Long conferences were held in which Mintz insisted his wife had some rights under the alleged option and Sullivan maintained she did not. It was agreed, however, that Sullivan enter into a new contract with Winkler Productions that would satisfy all concerned.

A trial was avoided when, on May 1, 1924, an agreement was signed between Winkler and Sullivan for the production of twenty-four Felix cartoons, of a minimum length of 650 feet, every two weeks for a year commencing May 15. The distributor agreed to increase Sullivan's payment to $2,400 for each negative. Peace was restored (for the time being) and the Felix films continued to be delivered without interruption.

Winkler happily announced (in *Moving Picture World* on May 10 and the next day in *The Film Daily*) the mutually acceptable agreement: "It affords me great pleasure to announce that the differences which have existed between Pat Sullivan, originator of the Felix Cartoon comics, and myself have been amicably adjusted."

Winkler's fiercely territorial advertisement effectively frightened off potential new distributors, and in order to maintain a steady flow of production and income, it was in Sullivan's best interests to resolve the conflict. The Mintzes wanted to settle the dispute in order to continue profiting from the most popular cartoon film series of the day.

The growing popularity of Felix emboldened both Otto Messmer and Hal Walker to marry their longtime fiancées in 1924. During 1924–1925, according to Hal Walker, the Sullivan studio "was put on a commercial production basis . . . I was told I could make more money if we produced more pictures."

With the contract settled in his favor financially and the expanded studio functioning well under Messmer's efficient and artistic supervision, Sullivan and his wife went to London for six weeks.

Winkler's sales of the films through Pathé in Europe had made Felix world-famous; in England, where the films appeared exclusively in

Mr. and Mrs. Pat Sullivan in London, May 21, 1924.

Pathé's *Eve & Everybody's Film Review*, a song, "Felix Kept On Walking," was written in 1923 and became one of the most popular songs of the day:

Felix keeps on walking, keeps on walking still.
With his hands behind him, You will always find him.
Blew him up with dynamite, But him they couldn't kill.
Miles up in the air he flew, He just murmured "Toodle-oo,"
Landed down in Timbuctoo
And kept on walking still.

The sheet-music cover for the most popular song in London in 1923. Collection of Mark Newgarden.

"I cannot remember," wrote a British reporter (for *Weston Super Mare* on May 14, 1924), "any cinema feature that has caught on quite like Felix, the fascinating black cat whose agitated whiskers and mobile ears have charmed so many millions to laughter. I admit that Felix is the one film star who intrigues me."

Film Daily of May 11, 1924 wrote of "The Felix Vogue" in England:

. . . the most popular song of the day is entitled "Felix Kept on Walking" and it is being sung by many music hall performers. There are Felix handkerchiefs, Felix toys, Felix chinaware, and an actor in vaudeville is made up to resemble Felix and struts in the same manner as Felix's peculiar little walk.

At the dock in Southampton aboard the liner *Berengaria*, Mr. and Mrs. Sullivan greeted the press. Photos of the couple—Marjorie smiling, wearing a cloche hat and fur-collared coat, Pat squinting in the sunlight, cigarette in hand, wearing a fedora, suit, vest, and tie topped by a scarf and overcoat—appeared in the *Birmingham Mail* and *Daily Sketch* under the heading "Creator of 'Felix.'"

Sullivan obliged the fourth estate by selectively recalling his difficult past ("Twelve years ago I was a no-account sort of comic artist in London"), and telling, for the first time, a quaint story that he would use over and over through the years to explain where Felix came from.

"I have earned all the cash for the Felix idea," said Sullivan, "but my wife has the credit. She came into my room one day carrying a stray cat—just an ordinary, back-garden, music-making, narrow-tailed,

85

unpedigreed sort of cat. 'Everybody cartoons men. Why not create an animal cartoon?'

"That was how Felix began. Now he is such an important figure in the world that I had to come to England personally for six weeks to attend to his business affairs. I tried to drop him once, but after a year he came back again, and has been with me ever since."

A reporter for the *Birmingham Mail* (on May 21, 1924) explained to readers, "Mr. Sullivan used to make 3,000 drawings for 660 feet of film when Felix began to amuse cinema audiences, but now he has to do 6,000 Felixes for the same length." The reporter was the first of many newsgatherers who blindly assigned all creative credit to Sullivan personally, neglecting to question why his lengthy absences from the studio had no effect on the clockwork delivery or the creative content of the Felix films.

Besides his fortnightly appearance on British movie screens, Felix's comic strip was published weekly. In addition, his image appeared in numerous publications and on objects. A newspaper writer from the town of Weston reported: "Nowadays you meet Felix everywhere in Weston. He figures in the shop windows as a mascot. Motorists display him in their bonnets [British term for a car's hood] to keep off police traps, and a few days ago actually I saw him mounting guard over the gardens at the Boulevard end of Orchard Street as a scarecrow." The writer mused about anthropologists in the year 3224 ("Britishologists") being puzzled upon finding Felix effigies and surmising that twentieth-century Britons were cat worshippers.

Sullivan was displeased to find that most of the published pieces and manufactured items bore neither Sullivan's name nor a copyright notice. *Picture Show* magazine of April 5, 1924, for example, offers to show readers "How Felix the Cat is made to walk," and features several illustrations of the cat inside and a larger one on the cover; but there

"Felix sneaks" in sequential animation drawings, c. 1923.

is no mention of Sullivan or his studio and no copyright indication. Likewise, the cover for the sheet music of "Felix Kept On Walking" features a poorly drawn, almost wolflike Felix walking hands-behind-back, but again Pat Sullivan's name does not appear nor does a copyright. At the top of the cover, however, the name of the distributor, Pathé, is prominently displayed.

The Sullivans attended the grand Wimbledon exposition, a major event in 1924, which was unofficially "changed to the Felix show, because there were so many stuffed cats modeled after [Felix] being carried around"; the king and queen tucked the dolls "under their arms." Sullivan was not amused. He noticed cats barely resembling Felix being called by his name, which he found "annoying, to say the least, especially as some of them are so inferior in intellect" and "looked as if they didn't know enough to wash their own faces."

Upset over the thought of losing income to copyright infringers and growing weary of the Felix hoopla, Sullivan gave a number of disgruntled interviews before leaving London. In one (which is unidentified in Sullivan's scrapbook except by the date May 29, 1924), he declared he "is tired of the cat . . . cannot shake it off, cannot travel anywhere but that it follows. On the voyage over he had to draw no fewer than 600 Felixes for fellow travelers, most of them 'hard-headed businessmen who ought to have known better.' "

In an unusual by-lined article (in another unidentified 1924 London newspaper article pasted into Sullivan's scrapbook), "What I Suffer from Felix," Sullivan complained that Felix was "coming perilously near getting a strangle-hold on my personality." His metaphor for Felix was monstrous: "An old German guy called Frankenstein once started something he could not finish. Well, I just feel like that about Felix. . . . I am introduced to somebody as Pat Sullivan. That makes no hit with anybody. Then the introducer has to make the usual crack: 'Well, you know Mr. Sullivan: he's the man who invented Felix.' Then there is some interest shown in me. They are mighty glad to have met me, and then comes the well-worn, time-honoured query: 'Say, and how did you think of it—lucky dog?' Interest in me from that moment ceases."

In the article, Sullivan again tells the now familiar public-relations

A cover story on Felix in London's *Picture Show* magazine, April 5, 1924.

In 1923, Winslow B. Felix, a Chevrolet dealer in Los Angeles at Eleventh and Olive, received permission from Pat Sullivan to use images of Felix in ads as a "firm mascot and trade character."

wash about how his wife brought him an alley cat and how it was the model for the famous Felix. At the end of his ill-tempered, self-pitying piece, Sullivan lodges a complaint about how "everyone in England is using" Felix.

American publicity man David Bader wrote on July 12, 1924, in an unidentified trade journal article about Felix's popularity and "exploitation in the United Kingdom":

> It is almost incredible, but the most popular outstanding figure in the film trade at this moment, throughout every nook and cranny of the Kingdom, is Felix the Cat. Never in my short but eventful life in the Film Industry have I ever seen anything to equal Felix's popularity, prestige and general screen personality. Honestly, our stars in the flesh are unknown in comparison and this is not putting it too strongly; to the contrary it is putting it mildly. There are

Felix songs, Felix tie pins, Felix brooches, Felix silver spoons, little and big Felix dolls, Felix pillow tops, Felix automobile radiator tops, Felix candy, Felix blankets, Felix street vendor novelties and more other publicity producing angles than a centipede has legs.

This is phenomenal in the face of the little press-agentry on the part of Pathe, who distributed [sic] Felix. Speaking to the manager of a Woolworth store, to whom I had introduced a Baby Peggy novelty, I queried if he thought it was possible to make a star in-the-flesh just as popular as Felix. He answered me, as frankly and as sincerely as a man can be, that he thought there was as much chance in doing that as there was in the Shenandoah [airship] flying to Mars. 'Nuff said, isn't it? That's how popular Felix is, and we can only say Margaret Winkler and clever Pat Sullivan are to be commended for having exported dear old Felix.

Upon his return to the States, Sullivan told Harry Kopp to demand Pathé Frères discontinue the collection of British merchandising royalties and to turn over to him all previous moneys earned from such royalties. A fight resulted between Pathé, Sullivan, and Margaret Winkler, which culminated in a tripartite agreement.

Kopp continued to arrange various Felix merchandising contracts in the States for Sullivan, including a Felix Crystal Radio Set that appeared in April, in which the tail formed the tuner and a solitary whisker was the crystal. On June 19, *Film Daily* announced that arrangements had been made with George Borgfeldt and Company to manufacture yet another Felix doll, to be retailed for one dollar at Liggett Drug Stores.

While in England, Sullivan also made the unpleasant discovery that Felix's films were not shown as full reels, but instead were fragmented into "chapter form." Sullivan described them in *The Cinema* (September 24, 1925) as "mutilated," and this discovery, plus the Pathé merchandise flap, fueled Sullivan's determination to rid himself of the Winkler organization as soon as the current contract was fulfilled.

If Sullivan needed one more nail for Winkler's coffin, he would find it in the form of a new cartoon series that the company began distributing to theaters in March 1924. The films, by a twenty-three-year-old newcomer on the West Coast—a transplanted midwesterner named Walt Disney—were a takeoff on Lewis Carroll's *Alice in Wonderland* and a reversal of Max Fleischer's *Out of the Inkwell* series (which Winkler also distributed). Instead of a cartoon character performing in the real world like Fleischer's Koko the Clown, young Disney presented a real little girl (named Alice) in a cartoon world.

The combination of live-action and animation in the same frame was expensive and tricky to do, so Alice appeared in openings and closings. The bulk of the film's action was dominated by one Julius, a circular black cat with a white mask, pointed ears, and a tail that "is certainly a versatile implement, as he proves in ALICE'S FISHY STORY (1924) . . . he uses his tail to cut through the ice and then as a fishing line."

Ever since Felix became popular, there had been Felix design clones and imitators of his mutable actions. In 1920, J. R. Bray, who previously had concentrated on human caricatures, suddenly presented "Thomas Cat" as the star of the first color cartoon, and Frank Moser's "Scat," who alternated with Felix on the *Paramount Magazine*, used question marks for props. In 1923, Paul Terry produced a plump black cat blatantly named "Felix," an appellation soon changed to "Henry Cat" after (it is assumed) Harry Kopp or Mintz-Winkler convinced him to do so.

Disney's Julius was especially galling, for it obviously plagiarized the design and actions of Sullivan's cat while sharing Sullivan's distributor. Recently, *Alice* animator Rudy Ising, in an interview with veteran Disney animator Frank Thomas, explained that it was Charles Mintz himself who requested that Disney's cartoonists "make their characters more like Felix."

"Felix was the successful character," wrote Thomas in a letter to this author, "and (cheap) producers have always been quick to get in on another creative person's success. [Mintz] asked that they use the 'gimmick' gags, like a fellow tips the whole of his head, ears and all, if he wants to tip his hat but isn't wearing one. Parts of the body can also be used whenever needed as a prop of any shape or design. Walt evidently didn't want to go very far in that direction for the very reason that those gags were associated with Felix. And when some of the fellows drew their cat [Julius] . . . to look too much like Felix, Walt

Members of Walt Disney's Hollywood studio in 1925. Standing, left to right: Walker Harman, Ubbe (Ub) Iwerks, Margie Gay (the second child to star in the *Alice* series), Walt Disney, and Rudy Ising. Kneeling, left to right: Isadore (Friz) Freleng, Roy Disney, and Hugh Harman. Collection of the author.

An advertisement for Disney's *Alice Comedies* series, c. 1924, featuring a Felix-like cat named Julius. Courtesy Robert and Katherine Fish.

said, and I quote Rudy, 'You'd better watch that stuff, fellows, you're going to run into copyright problems.'

". . . It was a loose operation and Walt had his hands full just trying to get a picture out on time with such an unskilled staff . . . more than one man on the crew thought it was smarter to listen to what [Mintz] said he wanted than to follow Walt. After all, he was only the kid who had been their neighbor back in Kansas City. What did he know?"

The tripartite contract between Sullivan, Winkler, and Pathé makes no mention of any rights that Winkler claimed in any heretofore existing option. So Sullivan and Kopp decided this agreement would be their escape hatch from further dealings with Winkler's company.

In February 1925, Harry Kopp formed Bijou Films, a corporation whose directors consisted of himself, his wife Lena, and Samuel Null, a partner in his law firm. This arrangement allowed Kopp as Sullivan's agent to profit directly from each film sale. All future Felix films would carry the screen credit "By Arrangement with The Bijou Films, Inc." which, as the producer of record, also provided protection for Sullivan against litigation.

Oh, Meow-w! That Funny Felix Hits Town With Famous Artist

Mr. and Mrs. Pat Sullivan, photographed in The Examiner Art Department yesterday shortl after their arrival from the East. Mr. Sullivan is known to millions as the creator of th world's comical cat, "Felix."

With only two months left on the current Winkler contract, Kopp sailed on the luxury liner *Leviathan* for England in March to negotiate with the Ideal Film Company, Ltd., for a new series of Felix short subjects to commence after the Winkler-Pathé contracts ran out. Kopp's youngest daughter, Erma, who was ten years old, accompanied her father on the trip and remembers the Ideal executives "were dying for the contract. They wined and dined us and at one London nightclub they whirled me, a ten-year-old, around the dance floor just to impress my father."

Kopp closed a contract with Ideal for Pat Sullivan by which terms he was to receive a whopping $5,000 for each of twenty-four Felix

subjects to be delivered two a month, the first due immediately after completion of the current contract with Winkler.

Back in New York, Kopp invited Charles Mintz to lunch, told him of the Ideal contract, and "asked him whether he would be interested in making a bid for the world rights to Felix other than England." Kopp mentioned that Joe Brandt was again interested in Felix and was offering $5,000 per film for the series, and if Mintz cared to offer an equal amount Kopp "would try to use my influence with Sullivan to see that he got the contract."

Mintz replied "he did not care to handle Felix any longer for the reason that Sullivan was asking entirely too much money for it and that the popularity of Felix had turned Sullivan's head and it was quite difficult for him to enter into [a] future harmonious relationship with him."

Harry Kopp, believing he had been up front with Mintz and the Winkler company regarding Sullivan's plans, proceeded to make a contract on behalf of his client and Bijou Films with the Educational Films Corporation of America and its president, Earle W. Hammons. Educational, a distribution company formed in 1915 whose motto/logo was "The Spice of the Program," promoted their films with splashy publicity. Full-page ads in the trades announced their coup signing Felix.

Mintz and Winkler immediately sued Sullivan, Kopp, Hammons, and Educational. In the court hearing that took place during the summer, Margaret Winkler as plaintiff pleaded in an affidavit that the contracts entered into by Sullivan with her in 1921 and 1922 were still in effect.

The court found in the defendants' favor, judging that when Winkler entered into a new contract with Sullivan it "covered the very subject matter of the alleged pre-existing option and if there had been any such option it would have become merged in the new contract."

The defendants crowed their triumph in an ad in the *Film Daily* dated August 3, 1925:

In view of the advertisements inserted in this paper by Margaret J. Winkler, "warning" the trade against making contracts with Pat

Sullivan for the exhibition and distribution of "Felix" cartoons, we beg to announce the following:

On the 25th day of July, 1925, the New York Supreme Court dismissed with costs, the action of Margaret J. Winkler to enjoin Pat Sullivan, Harry Kopp, Earl W. Hammons and the Educational Film Corporation of America.

The latest series of "Felix the Cat" being released by the Educational Film Corporation of America.

Pat Sullivan

The Mintzes refused to give up. They quickly entered an appeal, which was not heard by the court until January 1926 and was finally dismissed on April 26 of that year.

Charles Mintz grumbled about the Sullivan situation in one of his letters to Walt Disney dated October 6, 1925: "Haven't you a single spark of appreciativeness in your whole soul or are we going to face the same situation which we faced after having put a certain other short subject on the market only to have it proved a boomerang to us? . . ."

Winkler Productions soon produced a Disney film series starring Oswald the Lucky Rabbit, a character that was even more of a Felix the Cat clone than Julius. In 1928, when Disney asked for more money, Charles Mintz took the character, the series, and most of the cartoonist's staff away from him. Disney was forced to create a new character, which he named Mickey Mouse, and starred him in a "talkie" series that took the industry by storm. Pat Sullivan's slowness in adapting to the new sound technology pioneered by Disney would topple his studio.

Charles Lindbergh poses in
February 1929 in an F-3,
belonging to Fighter Squadron
2-B, with Felix emblazoned on
its side.

FELIX ON A HIGH ROLL, 1925–1928

A JAZZ BAND played Pat Sullivan's theme song, "Felix Kept On Walking," as he and Marjorie arrived in Southampton harbor aboard the White Star liner *Majestic*. Sullivan was unable to walk down the gangplank; he had to be carried, smiling and waving his hat, by stewards in an invalid chair to the London train.

"Two days before the Majestic sailed [on September 12, 1925]," explained a reporter from the *Bath & Wilts Chronicle*, "he was walking from his home in New York to his studio, when he was knocked over by a heavy lorry, which crushed his left foot and also injured the other. Mr. Sullivan had already booked his passage to England and although suffering a great deal of pain, decided not to cancel the trip."

Part celebration and part business, this five-month world tour began in London to officially kick off Sullivan's new contract with Ideal Film Company, Ltd. For the first time, Ideal would present Felix films in England in their full length, rather than as edited "chapters," as the previous distributor, Pathé, had done.

Ideal also made good on their promise to heavily promote Felix and Pat Sullivan in the British press. Even as the courts in America were deciding the fate of the Winkler-Sullivan contract in the summer of 1925, Ideal published in the July issue of the *Idealetter* a full-page image of Felix rubbing his hands with glee and standing above copy announcing: "The Cat—the whole cat—and nothing but the cat." Captions surrounding Felix brag confidently: "I'm off to Ideal as soon as Pat Sullivan finishes with my present guv'nors. I'm going to be a whole cat! I'm going to be a feature!"

In the August 13, 1925, *Kinematograph Weekly*, a trade magazine, Ideal placed a clever two-page ad: on the left page, behind bars in an oval frame, is Felix's tail. "This isn't all of me! . . . I shan't be happy until—" the copy says, leading the reader to the opposite page where the rest of Felix appears smiling and walking behind bars within another oval frame "—until I'm complete—a whole cat." "I'll be out in October," he assures us, as does Ideal's snappy slogan: "Millions will greet Felix complete."

The teasing Ideal print campaign continued in the September 3 issue of *Kinematograph Weekly*. One advertisement showed Felix happily "Bottled up till October" within a corked bottle labeled "The world's pick-me-up. A tonic for the blues. Not to be shaken. (Your patrons do the shaking.)"

Two examples of the promotional campaign of Ideal, Felix's distributor in London: (left) *The Idealetter*, July 1925, and (right) *Kinematograph Weekly*, September 3, 1925.

Pat Sullivan's personal appearance in London was an important component of Ideal's ballyhoo for the new Felix series. Despite the discomfort of a sore foot, he willingly and loquaciously held forth to the

press. "It's wonderful to be over here for a while," he told the *Illustrated Sunday Herald* (published on September 20). "London is so restful after New York. Here one can have peace at night, but over there it is impossible to get to sleep until about 4 A.M. on account of the incessant din of jazz bands, cabarets and pistol shots."

Sullivan boasted in *The Cinema* of September 24 that his new contract was "the highest sum ever paid for an animated cartoon," and he claimed the "new series of cartoons Ideal are putting out are better than ever, [because] instead of being shown in fragments, they will be shown in full." He claimed to be surprised that Britishers "have taken so enthusiastically to [Felix] in the old mutilated form."

At an Ideal-sponsored luncheon at the Savoy for "not a few seasoned exhibitors and hardened critics," Sullivan and his wife were honored guests. There, "a Felician atmosphere [was] created by Felix posters, Felix limericks, and the whole battery of 'artful aids' to publicity." Sullivan drew sketches of Felix after the latest "full-length" Felix film (*Felix the Cat Trips Through Toyland*) was screened, which "gave huge delight to the assembled company."

Kinematograph Weekly reviewed *Trips Through Toyland* most favorably in its October 15, 1925, issue:

Pat Sullivan, in a wheelchair with bandaged foot, relaxes with his wife at London's Savoy Hotel in September 1925.

> Felix holds an enviable position in kinemaland, inasmuch as he never grows old, and age only tends to improve him as a rare vintage of entertainment material. If the new Pat Sullivan cartoons are all as good as the first one shown, the public are in for a good time. In FELIX TRIPS THROUGH TOYLAND, they see the redoubtable black cat rescue a doll from a dog. The dog [*sic*] falls in love with its hero, and takes him into Toyland, where a villainous Pierrot is encountered. This bad man abducts Felix's beloved, and it is only after brilliant leadership of the Toy soldiers hair-breadth escapes and pitched battles that virtue triumphs. Workmanship is wonderful, there is no better entertainment than this to be had.

Toward the end of his London stay, Sullivan wearied of the daily parade of reporters, each asking the same questions and each requesting a sketch of Felix. He grew cranky in print (as he had the year before),

99

bemoaned his fate, and (again) likened Felix to a monstrous curse, rather than a bringer of good luck.

At about the same time in New York, a reporter paid a visit to the Sullivan studios. Since Pat Sullivan was in London, he talked with "the accommodating" Otto Messmer, the studio's "production manager," but he wrote his story as if he had also spent a day with Felix. Observing the busy animators and blackeners at work, the whimsical reporter admired "all these people who are doing such fascinating things with India ink," but it was "Felix" who showed him "stacks of sketches and a stunning panorama of clouds and castles: 'It's called FELIX FINDS THE RAINBOW'S END [released December 13, 1925], and it's the Cat's Meow! Here's me sliding down the rainbow and finding a pot of gold. Nice, eh? Though personally I would have preferred a pot of cream.' "

Interviews with "Felix," as well as by-lined articles "written" by the cartoon cat, were part of the media blitz Educational Pictures, Sullivan's American distributor, was conducting in tandem with Ideal on the other side of the Atlantic. There were even photo gimmicks that pictured Felix as an example of jazz-and-dance-mad youth: in the October 25, 1925, *New York Herald Tribune*, Felix dances the Charleston with Virginia Vance, of the "Educational-Mermaid Comedies." In another publication, "Felix decides that the Charleston is passé," and asks long-limbed Ann Pennington of George White's Scandals and the Ziegfeld Follies "for a lesson in the Black Bottom." According to Hal Walker, Miss Pennington posed in person for the cartoonists "in her best slow motion, so we could sketch Felix doing the same."

During Sullivan's months-long absence from New York, the Felix films continued to roll out of his studio and into theaters every two weeks. The quality of the Felix films released during this time was as high as that of any that preceded them; in fact, a number of them are among the best of the series.

Felix Trifles with Time, copyrighted October 13, 1925, for example, plays with metamorphosis and fantasy more boldly than ever before, resulting in a number of visual delights. Felix, looking as usual for a good meal, asks Old Man Time to travel back to "a better age." In a prehistoric setting, the scales on the back of a Gertie-like dinosaur

"Come on, cat! All set for the third step. Face forward, Felix, and bend that left knee slightly, pointing the left paw toward the floor. This is the way we make 'em sit up and take notice when we dance the 'Black Bottom' in Mr. White's 'Scandals' "

"Snap into the fourth step, funny feline! Stamp that left mouse-catcher on the floor and bend that left knee. Stamp it good and hard. And sing that song—'They call it Black Bottom, a new twister. They sure got 'em, oh sister!' "

Ziegfeld Follies star Ann Pennington teaches the Black Bottom to Felix in 1925.

become an escalator; another prehistoric creature, a combination stego-saurus and hound, looks like an in-between drawing of an incomplete metamorphosis; a lovely shape from a geyser splash quickly turns into a parachute for a safe landing.

The irrational invincibility of all animated cartoons is well repre-sented here by Felix, who survives a miles-high fall with only an easily reattached broken leg; his slow descent from close-up to distant dot predicts the future falls of Chuck Jones's Coyote in the Warner Brothers *Roadrunner* series. Felix also survives a flaying, and until he battles a caveman for the return of his fur, his intact round head rests on a tiny skeleton, a disturbing sight that brings to mind Mardi Gras death cos-tumes. The meaning of words is also played with, as seen in the film's final dialogue card (of which there are few compared to the earlier Felix cartoons): time-traveler Felix returns from the Stone Age and, happy to root around for food again in trash cans in modern-day 1925,

101

declares he prefers "the Garb-Age." In the opening of *Trifles with Time*, hungry Felix chews on a shoe, a bit of pathos borrowed from the famous shoe-eating scene of Felix's "mentor" Charlie Chaplin in his feature *The Gold Rush*, released in August.

Felix the Cat in the Cold Rush (released November 1) parodies the title of Chaplin's film and its story. Hungry Felix attempts to escape a gun-toting human (as Chaplin did a similarly armed Mack Swain) by jumping into a refrigerator. Now cold as well as hungry, he hallucinates (alternating frames of black and white circles and settings) and thinks that he is in the frozen North ("In Hot Water," reads an ironic full-screen card). There he battles, Chaplin-like, for his life against the elements (he is always cold), men (angry Eskimos), and beasts (a polar bear and a seal).

Chaplin supposedly once said he envied the perfect timing of gags in animated cartoons, attributing it to the fact that cartoons never had to take the time to breathe. Felix finds solutions to problems well beyond those available to Chaplin, who, for all the magical control he had over his wonderful body, was finally limited simply because he was part of the physical world. Felix, the lively illusion from an artificial

Pat, Felix, and Marjorie in
Circulation magazine,
September 1925.

| Sketch of Background — the "still-life" portion which is used throughout in the series, but not redrawn | Single sketch of "animated" portion only, for use in combination with the prepared "still-life" background. | The Combination of prepared "still-life" setting and preceding "animated" sketch, now ready for the camera. | A subsequent Combination in the series prepared for the camera. A succession of "animated" sketches, each a trifle different from its predecessor, has led up to the present distinct change. |

A sequence from "How a Moving Film Drawing Is Made," from the August 4, 1923, *Illustrated London News*.

world, has no physical limitations: he escapes a melting igloo by climbing aboard a delicately animated wisp of smoke; exclamation points, symbols of Felix's thoughts, are transformed into forceps to remove a walrus's sore tusks, which in turn become skis for Felix.

"Appearance is the sole reality here," wrote Bela Balazs in 1945 of the Felix films, "and art is not made into reality. When Felix the Cat bends his tail into the shape of a wheel, he can already roll away on it. No need for it to turn into the reality of a wheel. A drawn wheel is good enough for a drawn cat. In Sullivan's drawn world there are no miracles; for in it there are only lines and these function according to the shape they take on." In *Eats Are West* (November 15), cowboy Felix forms his lariat into the shape of a horse, which fills in its form to become a bucking bronco; with Felix on its back, the horse gallops away, but the frantic pace of the chase gradually reverts the horse to a mere stick figure again, an excellent example of Balazs's dictum that "in the world of creatures consisting only of lines the only impossible things are those which cannot be drawn."

The production of animated cartoons is too complicated a process to be dictated long-distance, or, as Pat Sullivan claimed, by merely leaving "key drawings" behind for his staff to follow; it is an art and a craft that requires constant supervision and direct artistic input. Sullivan's vague explanations of how this was possible without his presence— e.g., in the December 1 issue of *The Argus*: "I have left enough material in America to enable my staff to produce the fortnightly picture for some months to come . . ."—satisfied the press and in turn the public,

103

who regarded animation as one of life's great mysteries. Basically, both were uninterested in looking beyond the public relations smoke screen to really find out what (and who) made Felix tick.

The Felix films are consistently great because Otto Messmer held a tight rein on the creation of each one. Though produced via a studio system involving many hands, the films and their star were essentially extensions of Messmer's personality and a manifestation of his unique creative mind.

"Otto was all-round," recalled animator and former Felix blackener Al Eugster. "Besides animating, as the animators finished their scenes or sequences, he would give them more work. He would, in a sense, be directing the picture. We didn't use that term then.

"[The script] just came out of Otto's head and it never seemed to get on paper somehow. There never seemed to be any conference. Otto would get an idea or a subject. He probably made notes, but there was no, what we call, a formal script. He would have a pretty good idea of what he wanted and he would convey it to the animator, but it seemed to be done on an individual basis. Everything that was animated went right into final production. The animator would just discuss it with him on an individual basis and would pick up this scene or sequence and go ahead and animate it. Then it would be passed down to the end, where we would ink it and blacken it."

Eugster, who later animated for Max Fleischer and Walt Disney, began his career at age sixteen at the Sullivan studio on April Fools' Day in 1925. He left four years later almost to the day and is one of two surviving participants (Hal Walker is the other) in the making of the films during Felix's years of peak popularity—the Educational-Ideal period.

He was paid ten dollars a week, nine dollars less than he earned doing odd jobs at American Radiator Company, but "it was something I wanted to do." When Eugster left the studio in 1929, his salary was twenty-five dollars a week.

The animators and blackeners sat on straight-backed chairs with pillows at desks lined in a row against one wall of the loft; Pat Sullivan's private office was opposite them. A shaded window was near the animators and a large window faced West Sixty-third Street in the front

of the long room; in a darkened area behind Sullivan's office was Alfred Thurber and the animation camera and lights. A partition separated the back area, which contained a toilet, a table, chairs, and another window. The only decorative touch was paper Felix posters pinned to the walls.

The animation desks contained two shelves to hold paper, pencils, pens, and other materials. Pencil sharpeners were attached to the desks and so were small light bulbs for extra illumination should the ceiling lamps prove inadequate on overcast days. A square opening cut into the slanted top of each desk held a glass; underneath, a light enabled the animators to see through several sheets of paper as they drew Felix and friends in progressive poses atop the glass. Two wooden pegs at the top of the drawing board held the paper drawings (each punched with two holes) in register.

Advertisements for (right) the Felix comic strip and (left) a new doll featuring Felix in a dress!

The animation was drawn mainly on paper, and by 1925 the Barre system of slash-and-tear was not used; instead, cels containing backgrounds were placed over the character drawings. This method was inexpensive because of the limited use of cels, but it required special planning by the animators in order to avoid having Felix appear to walk through horizon lines or objects. The animators drew nonmoving elements on a cel, which was placed over the character action drawings on paper. If Felix's movements made him cross the lines of the horizon or objects, the cel overlay was removed and the horizon line or the object was carefully traced onto each of the paper drawings containing the character.

Characters were rarely inked onto cels at Sullivan's, except for special scenes, e.g., in front of a dark background or for a repeated cycle on a pan background. The camera was an ancient Bell & Howell 35 and it was stationary; movements into and out of the camera field were mechanically impossible and had to be drawn. "Everything was set," said Eugster, "and they worked on one field, which was confining." But Messmer and company found creative solutions to the technical problems: Felix often three-dimensionalizes an action by dynamically bringing it from a far distance to close range, and even "wipes" one scene into another by moving so close to the "camera" that his black body obliterates the view.

About 2,500 to 3,000 drawings were required per each six-minute Felix short; in order to organize and communicate the number of film frames to be photographed for each drawing, today's animation studios use charts called "exposure sheets." At Sullivan's, Eugster recalled, "we didn't use exposure sheets. The number of frames to be exposed for each drawing was written on that particular drawing (outside the camera field), such as 1X (one frame), 2X, etc., or hold for 16X, and so on. Any additional notes were written on a separate sheet of paper." The positioning of the levels of paper and cels under the camera was "no problem": on the bottom was the paper drawing, on the top was the cel containing the inked background, and in between was an extra cel, if needed.

The studio was a pleasant working place, quiet, except for the clicking of Mr. Thurber's camera shutter as the men and boys worked over

Camera

THE ILLUMINATED EASEL
with frosted glass plate,
enables the artist to indicate
on his paper placed over
preceding sketch, the new
progressive lines wanted

in the field of the camera lens.

Camera

Framing Device ↑

(2) Making a
successive picture.

their drawing boards. There were no women inkers at Sullivan's during Felix's heyday.

The craft of animation often requires intense concentration. Eugster recalled once literally "sweating away on a very difficult drawing. I was inking this oval, and Pat [Sullivan] brought [a] visitor over and he mentioned, 'You've got to have pretty steady nerves to do that.' Of course, I was hoping they would just go away, so I could finish this thing. My nerves were never that steady." The blackeners dipped flexible crow-quill pens into bottles of black India ink and carefully traced over the animator's original pencil drawings. Brushes were used to blacken in characters. "Then we'd have to erase the pencil lines," said Eugster. "That was a mean job, if I had a large job to blacken in. That was sort of monotonous—blackening. But it was part of cartoons, so I accepted it."

Sometimes Eugster became bored with filling in Felix's form and would furtively draw tiny cartoons of his own devising inside Felix's lines before blackening them in. While waiting for the animators to give them work, the young blackeners would go to the back area to gaze out the window or they would play baseball with a mailing tube and a wad of paper; the paper, said Eugster, went "flying over the partition . . . and I think one time it landed on Mr. Thurber's camera field, and we still like to think he photographed the paper."

To Eugster, Otto Messmer was "Mr. Felix the Cat, himself. Synonymous with Felix." Besides all his creative duties, "every Friday Otto would go to the bank and pick up the payroll and we would get paid."

Eugster recalled that during his four years at the studio he didn't see much of Pat Sullivan, who would come in occasionally and go into his private office.

"Pat Comes Home," said the headline in the December 4, 1925, Sydney, Australia, *Daily Guardian*; "A Black Cat for Luck/Felix—Fortune" said the subhead of a classic rags-to-riches news story:

Dad!
Pat Sullivan, junior, the cartoonist, dashed down the gangway, grabbed Pat Sullivan, senior, and kissed him.

Marjorie Gallagher Sullivan in London, 1925.

A little later, when dad and the others had come aboard the [liner] Narkunda, Pat Sullivan, senior, was grabbed by a little yellow-haired blonde with both arms and hugged and kissed some more.

A photo accompanying the article, titled "Likes her daddy-in-law," shows Marjorie Sullivan widely grinning toward the camera, cheek by jowl with Pat Sullivan's blind father, whom she is holding in a tight embrace.

"I'm that excited I can hardly talk," said the creator of Felix the Cat, who has picked up a slight American accent on his sojourn abroad. Five years ago Pat Sullivan paid a visit to Australia. His father is a cab proprietor at Darlinghurst. Pat was not famous then, and came and went unheralded.

But today—

"Felix is the biggest sensation in the States and England," he declared. "It was a damned hard struggle, though.

"I've slept on the Thames Embankment, and in cheap New York lodging houses. But I got there. I guess I had the old dad's tenacity, and that pulled me through," he added with a glance at his father.

And Dad smiled back at the son who made good.

This article about Sullivan's return to his homeland was eventually cut and pasted, along with numerous examples of the publicity generated by Mr. and Mrs. Sullivan's world tour, into two scrapbooks Sullivan kept, titled "What they say about Felix." The scrapbooks vividly demonstrate the international fame Felix and Sullivan were enjoying by 1925: a Sullivan sketch of Felix with a bandaged foot was published in Liège, Belgium, in *La Meuse*, November 27, 1925 ("Pied cassé ou pied non cassé, je continuerai à marcher, n'importe comment"); a report from the December 5, 1925, *South African Pictorial* in Johannesburg stated, "The 'Felix' series of films have met with such success that an entirely new series of adventures of that astounding cat have started on the African Theatres, Ltd. screens"; in Germany, the *Berliner Tageblatt*, May 17, 1925, analyzed Felix and "Der Absolute Film" (in 1929, *Film Kurier*, the German equivalent of *Variety*, would list Felix as the greatest animation star of his times); a photo from the *Shanghai Times* of December 27, 1925, shows 180 children enjoying a Chinese conjurer and "a Felix the Cat cinema show"; Sullivan's scrapbook also contains a clipping from a Chinese-language newspaper with a large photo of himself in the middle of the page.

In March 1926, the Sullivans finally returned to New York.

Nearly a dozen new Felix cartoons had been produced by Messmer during Sullivan's absence and Felix was a hotter property than ever. Sullivan and Harry Kopp sought to exploit Felix through aggressive marketing of his image. First, they protected their valuable property by suing any manufacturer who used Felix's image without permission. "With the increase in the popularity of Felix," explained *Cartoons and Movies Magazine* in June 1927, "human nature ran true to form when a number of firms manufacturing various novelties decided they would use Felix or, at least, the nearest thing to him that could be designed without fear of court proceedings, to accelerate their business interests. Each and every one of these gentlemen has been whipped along the injunction line until today Pat Sullivan is sitting pretty, his ownership for all time of his brain child established by the highest courts in the land."

Plush-cloth Felix dolls by Chad Valley and possibly Steiff. Courtesy Christie's East.

Felix was licensed to appear on at least two hundred toys of various sizes manufactured internationally, from mechanical sparklers to waddling figurines; his image adorned articles of clothing and was featured in books and on items as diverse as cigars and baby oil. For his permission, Pat Sullivan was paid a royalty on a percentage basis; however, several deals, such as Felix pencils and pencil boxes made by the American Lead Company, were the result of oral agreements with Sullivan. This arrangement effectively cut out paying contract negotiating fees to attorney Kopp, who became aware of this practice only after Sullivan's death.

"There are many Felix toys and other manufactured products paying regular royalties to Mr. Sullivan," commented *Cartoon and Movies Magazine*. "During the very warm summer months when they say business is poor, the writer saw a month's royalty check for nearly $1,500—a fairly good incidental earning germinating from a dilapidated alley cat."

On May 9, 1927, King Features began running (with Sullivan's blessing) a daily Felix comic strip in addition to the Sunday strip, which Messmer continued to draw. The cartoonist for the daily Felix was Jack Bogle, "one of my boys," said Hal Walker, "hired as an eraser and blackener. . . . Jack was assigned to cut out pictures of Felix and paste them in blocks for the strip. The story (balloons) came from Otto, Jack and the rest of the animators."

The Sullivan staff now included Dana Parker, an animator who also relieved busy Otto Messmer of the task of designing the bimonthly Felix film poster. (A discreet "DP" initialed on each poster identifies his work.) Bill Nolan left in mid-1925 to revive a *Krazy Kat* film series for Charles Mintz and was replaced by George Stallings, who went on in the 1930s to become a storyman at Disney's.

He was followed in the "guest animator" spot by none other than Raoul Barre, the man who gave both Pat Sullivan and Hal Walker (and so many others) their start in the animation business. Barre had fallen on difficult times in both his business and his personal life, and Sullivan responded to his plight with a job offer. Barre only stayed at the studio for about six months, but his experience and talent were appreciated by Messmer and added considerably to films such as *Felix*

Jack Bogle, cartoonist of the daily Felix comic strips, about 1927.

111

the Cat in Two Lips Time (August 22, 1926), *Felix the Cat Shatters the Sheik* (September 19), *Felix the Cat Hunts the Hunter* (October 3), *Felix the Cat Trumps the Ace* (November 28), and *Felix the Cat Dines and Pines* (January 9, 1927).

"It was quite a thrill to work with something that you know is 'going,' " said Otto Messmer of Felix's phenomenal success. Nineteen twenty-seven has been called the high tide of the twenties, and popular Felix gaily rode the crest of its wave; his films continued to delight audiences with their wide-ranging fantasy, visual wit, and contemporary references.

"At last, here was the symbol of our generation scrambling to realize its wild dreams in absurdities, such as defying gravity," wrote M. Paule in *Hollywood Life* in January 1927. "There was the airplane, the submarine and the Charleston. Felix of the form plastic could manipulate that war dance as no living human with two legs. In sum here was in Felix the Cat the Delphic oracle and a world horoscope rolled all into one."

In *Pedigreedy* (released January 23, 1927), outcast Felix lives in a barrel and dresses himself in the morning by literally pulling himself together: putting his lower legs on as if they were a pair of pants, donning his ears like a hat, and as a crowning touch, taking the question mark that emerges from his head and popping it onto his rear end to become his curvy tail. Seeking entry to the exclusive "400 Club," Felix must first prove his "unquestionable lineage" to a haughty headwaiter. The tale he spins traces his ancestry to two cats on Noah's ark (the twin Felixes save the biblical patriarch from drowning by forming a ladder made from multiples of themselves), a Pharaoh's pet (who teaches the Egyptian king to Charleston so frenetically that he explodes and Felix assumes his place on the throne), and Columbus's adviser (proving the shape of the earth by throwing a brick, Ignatz-like, around the planet that ends up hitting the Italian explorer in the head).

In *Felix the Cat Hits the Deck* (December 11), Messmer experiments with real objects moved frame by frame under the camera; in this case, it is a deck of playing cards, which chases Felix through an Alice-in-Wonderland world, tossing off poker-faced puns all the way: "Felix led

113

the ace"; "That's the King's auntie. I'll work her for some Jack."; "Hungry in a strange land, with the cards stacked against him."

Flim Flam Films (September 18) finds Felix and his three kittens barred from entering a movie theater (where, ironically, he is starring on the screen). After walking and thinking (while the kits cry geysers of tears), Felix decides to steal a clothing dummy and disguise the four cats as one tall man in a long coat (one kitten becomes a derby and its tail the dummy's mustache). The ruse fails, and they are tossed out but finally enter the movie palace through the electric wiring, emerging in globular lighting fixtures. The kits, at first, are thrilled to discover that the film stars Felix ("Look, there's Daddy!"), but become upset when the movie cat is attacked by a movie bear. To save "Felix," they jump from the balcony onto the large sheet that is the screen, with the real Felix following. The outraged audience throws the cats out and Felix placates his brood by suggesting they make their own home movies.

At "the first showing" for Felix's wife, Felix and the kits proudly screen shots of an "outdoor dancing school" (with wonderful "distorted-lens" animation of a hefty Isadora-like dancer by Raoul Barre), a parade (mistakenly shot upside down), and a bathing-beauty cat posing. Felix pops into the frame of the home movie (as if the camera were stopped and started abruptly), flirts with and kisses the beauty, the last shots photographed by the kittens without Felix's knowledge. In a jealous fury, Mrs. Felix knocks the projector over and a violent silhouetted fight leaves Felix in bandages and an arm cast, gesturing to us to stop filming him and iris out to end the movie.

Flim Flam Films, subtle and clever in its reflection of the movie-making process, is one of only two overtly self-referential Felix cartoons that Messmer ever made. In the other, *Comicalamities* (April 1, 1928), Messmer would experiment with bringing the "hand of the artist" into the frame to draw Felix and contribute directly to his adventures, a convention of self-figuration he had not used since the title opening of *Felix Saves the Day* eight years before. "Messmer no longer feels obligated to physically enter the image," explains Donald Crafton. "Instead, he enters the film through total identification with the character."

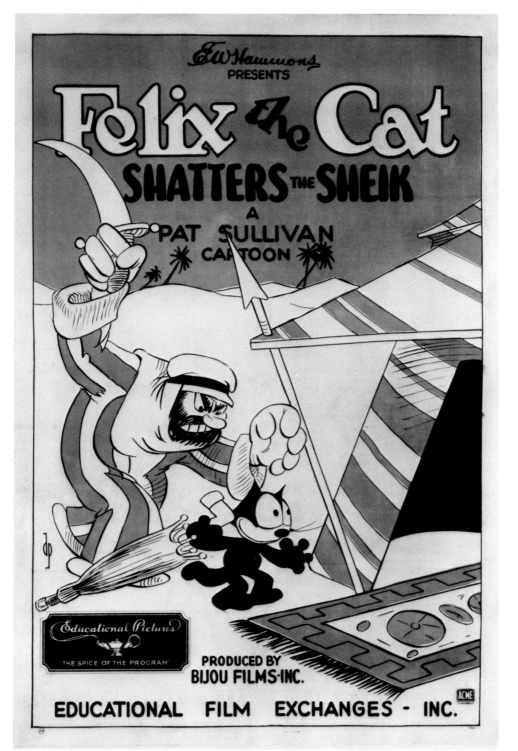

Flim Flam Films again portrays marriage as war or at least a mine-field of misunderstanding, a theme repeated in *Whys and Otherwhys* (November 27), where Felix drunkenly tries to put a key in a lock quietly (to avoid confronting his wife), with the balletic grace of Chaplin's similar attempt to gain entry to his home in *One A.M.* (1916). In the twenties, Felix is often shown in a number of films whooping it up and drinking in a Prohibition-defying speakeasy.

"You've got to consider the era we were living in," wrote Ben Harrison, producer of a *Krazy Kat* film series in the 1920s, in a letter. "PROHIBITION. Where people who now-adays pride themselves on the number of credit cards they carry, in those days, it was the number of Speakeasy cards you owned. The favorite game was how far uptown you could get and still stand up, starting at 42nd St., and Broadway. Nobody ever made Columbus Circle. That was Indian country."

A film frame from *Felix Dines and Pines* (1927). Courtesy Donald Crafton.

Before tying the knot, Felix's woman is a passive if fickle love object, who needs to be diligently wooed and won; after marriage, she becomes a suspicious harridan, armed with a rolling pin and ready to do battle with Felix, the irresponsible, philandering, lying husband.

Romance and the joy of sexual pursuit are the domain of the bachelor; in the breezy *Romeeow* (May 15), a dashing Felix rises to his ladylove's balcony on an exhaust vapor from his motor scooter, scoops ice cream for her from a nearby cumulus cloud, and caterwauls love songs after changing his tail into a strumming banjo. Such amorously fanciful scenes never happen between the sexes when Felix is shown to be married and saddled with responsibilities, such as children.

Starting in mid-1927, a number of plots in Felix films revolve around speedy travel, the traversing of wide distances, and aeronautical derring-do. This was a direct response to an event that has come to symbolize the spirit of the twenties: Charles Lindbergh's solo flight across the Atlantic Ocean from New York to Paris. "The entire Western world seemed suspended—and unified—by a tiny airplane somewhere over the Atlantic," wrote Geoffrey Perrett. "For an entire generation the most memorable day in their lives was the day they heard that Lindbergh had crossed the coast of France. . . . There had never been a triumph like it. There has not been one since."

About a month after Lindbergh's flight, Messmer and crew artfully imitated life in *Felix the Cat in "Loco" Motive* (released on June 26). Raymond Ganley reviewed the film on July 29 for *Motion Picture News*:

> The news prints are full these days of recountals [*sic*] of the various American flying expeditions over long stretches of ocean to some spot thousands of miles away from our own shores. Now, when most everyone talks and thinks of aviation, the wide awake Pat Sullivan and staff send Felix to Europe in an airship of his own devising. As is nine times out of ten the case with Felix, his thoughts and ambitions were sent winging Germany way because of hunger. When he beholds a well-nourished Teuton, the cat concludes that Germany must be a land overflowing with milk and honey. And so it is not long afterward that he faces Eastward and sets out to conquer the air. Though he meets many obstacles and conquers them one by one, your sympathies are with the lone cat flying over a waste of water. A really good cartoon storm, pelting rain, dark, threatening clouds, a veritable downpour with thunder and lightning, hits the intelligent feline but he manages to stay up in the air and continue his trip, arriving in Germany where a great multitude awaits him. . . .

The next month saw the release of *Felix the Cat in the Travel-Hog* (July 24), in which Felix slips on a bar of soap, falls out a window, is in turn kicked by a mule into the path of a passing tornado and whirled around the globe, and finally lands on the moon!

In *The Non-Stop Fright* (August 21), Felix most strongly aligns himself with the courageous Lindbergh. Swept up like trash and thrown out of a house by a thoughtless maid, homeless Felix wanders and comes upon a newspaper. A nearby signpost saying "478 miles" provides Felix with a chair (an upside-down 4), a pipe (a sideways 7), and eyeglasses (the number 8). He reads of an offer of a $50,000 prize for the "first to arrive" in "Timbuctoo" [*sic*]. (Lindbergh received a $25,000 prize put up by a French hotelier.)

Felix decides to fly to western Africa and creates the fuselage of his flying machine (as flimsy as the *Spirit of St. Louis*) from a barrel; the wings are two EAT AT JOE'S sandwich boards snatched from a salesman

117

who fell into a manhole (opened and placed in his way by Felix); the whirling propeller is formed from the "dizzy" symbols swirling around the salesman's head after his fall.

Lindbergh's thirty-six-hour life-and-death battle with rainstorms and fatigue is caricatured by Felix. He literally fights with storm clouds, duels with lightning, and rides a cloud horse to catch up with his runaway airplane. Plunged into the sea, Felix escapes an octopus and a piscine patrolman, whose motorcycle wheels are formed by two eels. Felix finds no relief in Timbuktu: animals and cannibals alike chase him with murderous intent. By pulling the skin off an elephant (as if it were a pair of long johns) and blowing it up like a balloon with his own breath, Felix escapes his tormentors in another flying machine, one from a quieter, slower era than the speed-mad 1920s.

In October, aviatrix Ruth Elder attempted to cross the Atlantic solo, five years before Amelia Earhart. For good luck, she carried a Bible, a Chinese ring, and a stuffed Felix doll (it has often been erroneously reported that Lindbergh carried a Felix doll); newspaper photos show

Elder clutching the doll to her bosom. After crashing in midocean, Elder was rescued, but Felix was not. Pat Sullivan, quick to see the publicity value in the situation, sent Elder a cable: "Am all right. Swam ashore. Will see you soon—Felix." When a new doll came in the mail, Elder again posed with it for newspapers, claiming, "Luck saved me."

That same month, *Felix the Cat Switches Witches* (October 2)—in which flight is again featured, this time on a broom—was screened by the National Board of Review and selected for the *Photoplay Magazine* Guide of Popular Entertainment films with a listing in the October issue.

In 1927, Sacco and Vanzetti died in the electric chair; Wayne B. Wheeler, head of the Anti-Saloon League and Prohibition crusader, died of exhaustion trying to save the country from booze; Texas Guinan, oft-arrested speakeasy owner, starred in a Broadway musical called *Padlocks of 1927*; Jack Dempsey quit the ring; and Babe Ruth ("the Sultan of Swat") hit sixty home runs in 154 games for the Yankees. Something else happened that busy year: the premiere of the Warner Brothers' all-singing, all-talking full-length feature film *The Jazz Singer*, an event that truly put the roar into the Roaring Twenties.

DOWN AND OUT, 1928–1933

BEFORE *The Jazz Singer*," wrote Neal Gabler in *An Empire of Their Own*, "Hollywood waited. After *The Jazz Singer*, the rush to sound began." The Warner Brothers feature starring Al Jolson was not the first attempt to merge moving pictures with sound; there had been numerous experiments through the years, including Warner's *Don Juan* in 1926. *Don Juan*, the first full-length sound movie, had music and sound effects, but not the spoken word. Audiences were impressed, but the industry waited to see if sound tracks were merely a novelty or truly the wave of the future. *The Jazz Singer*, which premiered in New York on October 6, 1927, provided the definitive answer.

"It more than revivified the sound movement," said Gabler. "By ad-libbing a few lines, Jolson had made it the first feature film with speech and introduced a whole new set of possibilities." The day after *The Jazz Singer* opened, producers on both coasts began scrambling to change over their studios and films to sound technology.

Walt Disney was not the first producer to use sound with animated cartoons. Through the 1920s, the Fleischer brothers experimented with optional De Forest Phonofilm sound tracks for their *Song Car-tunes*. Paul Terry, who had produced over two hundred silent Aesop's Fables for producer Amadee Van Beuren, produced a synchronized sound film titled *Dinnertime*, three months before Disney's *Steamboat Willie* starring Mickey Mouse. Terry's short, announced in *Motion Picture World* on August 18, 1928, "has been synchronized with the RCA Photophone. All the animals of the jungle as pen-and-inked in animation in

Opposite: Felix seems to fear the sounds made by a 1920s radio, a premonition of his own fate at the arrival of sound movies.

DISNEY CARTOONS
present a
MICKEY MOUSE
SOUND CARTOON
"STEAMBOAT WILLIE"
A WALT DISNEY COMIC
by UB IWERKS
RECORDED BY Powers CINEPHONE SYSTEM
MM-1

Aesop's Fables will enunciate aloud in their more or less natural 'voices.' . . . A background of orchestral music is offered throughout the reel."

Walt Disney saw a preview of *Dinnertime* in September at RCA, when he was making the rounds of New York recording companies seeking equipment to put a sound track on *Steamboat Willie*. His reaction to the film was included in a letter to his brother in Los Angeles: "MY GOSH—TERRIBLE—A lot of racket and nothing else. I was terribly disappointed. I really expected to see something halfway decent. BUT HONESTLY—it was nothing but one of the rottenest fables I believe I ever saw, and I should know because I have seen almost all of them. It merely had an orchestra playing and adding some noises. The talking part does not mean a thing. It doesn't even match. We sure have nothing to worry about from these quarters."

By November, both Van Beuren and Charles Mintz announced their studios would convert totally to sound productions, though the shorts were really postsynchronized silent films.

Disney was right: after November 18, he had nothing to worry about from competitors. *Steamboat Willie*'s debut (which was also the first public appearance of Mickey Mouse) changed not only Disney's life but the animation industry as well.

Disney's sound short was hailed by both public and press. *New York Daily Review* of November 18 recognized the film as "the first animated cartoon made especially for sound production, and as such it illustrates the perfection of synchronization that is possible when pictures are constructed especially for sound accompaniment."

After a two-week run at the Colony Theatre, *Steamboat Willie* moved to the grand Roxy Theatre. Disney remained in New York to meet with potential distributors and to add sound to three other Mickey Mouse films. Since most of his Los Angeles staff had left him to work for Charles Mintz, Disney attempted to recruit experienced animators from the East Coast. To this end, he visited a number of Manhattan animation shops, including the Pat Sullivan studio.

Hal Walker recalled "the day that Walt Disney came and tried to steal Otto away from the Sullivan studios. The conversation was such that Otto said he would think about it, but he wasn't convinced it was a good move for him."

Opposite: A poster for Walt Disney's *Steamboat Willie*, starring Mickey Mouse, which premiered November 18, 1928, at New York's Colony Theatre. © Walt Disney Pictures.

Others on Sullivan's staff were not so reluctant to leave. Burt Gillett was an experienced animator, having worked at Barre's, the Hearst studio, and Fleischer's. But he had never really fit in. According to Hal Walker, when Disney asked Messmer to join his studio in Los Angeles, "Gillett overheard all of the conversation and anticipated the time of Walt's departure and he went out ahead of Walt and met him and said, 'I'm your man!' " Gillett became part of Disney's studio in April 1929 and in 1933 directed Disney's *Three Little Pigs*, a triumph of "personality" animation and the most renowned cartoon film of the Depression years.

"It was pressure!" said Messmer about Disney's job offer. "He begged and pleaded. But my home, family, and roots were in New York. And besides, it looked like Felix would go on forever. He was at the height of his success."

In 1928, Felix did indeed maintain his status as one of the movies' most popular stars. Once again he was celebrated in popular song, this one a jazzy tune with corny lyrics written and published in America:

> There's a cat, a fuzzy creature. In the movies he's a feature
> He's some Cat. All the kiddies and the mammas,
> Say that he's the "cat's pajamas." He's all that.
> When on the screen he appears,
> They shout these words in his ears.
> Felix Felix Felix the Cat.
> Welcome welcome welcome home to our flat
> You fascinate me with your funny meow
> I'll feed you catnip and sweet milk from the cow
> Felix Felix in our backyard
> You can hang up your hat
> Make your pillow underneath a pussywillow
> Felix Felix the cat.

That same year, Paul Hindemith wrote a score, *Felix at the Circus*, to be presented at the Baden-Baden festival. Felix animator Dana Parker, who before the war appeared on the stage with Lew Telegren and Lasky Films, wrote an article for the January 1928 issue of *Theatre* magazine about bringing to life Felix and other pencil and pen "actors":

Often the question is put, "How is it done?" and any adequate answer seems so technical as to be likely to bore the questioner, who will regret his curiosity. Often, at the end of a painstaking explanation of the uses of "cels," "slashes," "repeats," "pans," and "exposure sheets," the animator is greeted with the question: "Yes, I understand all that, but how do you make them move?"

In the summer of 1928, in a mid-Manhattan studio, a twelve-inch papier-mâché statue of Felix was placed on a phonograph turntable and bathed in hot, bright lights before the first RCA TV camera. Felix was selected for his recognizability and his strong, simple black-and-white design, and perhaps because he was known as a good-luck charm. Felix whirled around for hours, as technicians made adjustments and refinements on their camera. Some months later, a crude sixty-line television picture of black-and-white Felix was transmitted to Kansas. The image, containing so many horizontal line imperfections it looked like Felix was being shot through venetian blinds, was picked up by

NBC tests the first RCA television camera on a rotating Felix doll in 1928.

video buffs at points in between New York and Kansas on primitive receivers. (Ironically, Felix would eventually be replaced by a Mickey Mouse doll for television testing purposes.)

The quality of the Felix films in 1928 was as good as that of any which preceded them. The inventiveness of the visual gags remained high and wild, the plots far-flung. In *Astronomeows* (July 8), Felix attaches himself to an arrow and flies to Saturn, where he interrupts an apparently perpetual bicycle race on the planet's ring; he saves the planet Mars and its strange inhabitants (one, a hammerheaded creature that pounds Felix into the ground like a black nail) by punching an errant comet back into outer space. In *Arabiantics* (May 13), Felix rides a flying carpet to the Persian Gulf in search of stolen jewels, transforms himself into a chair to invade a harem, and, after mice push him from a minaret, splats into sixteen tiny black balls that immediately reform into a whole Felix.

The formula of the Felix films was loose and broad enough (Felix hungry, Felix homeless, Felix loveless, etc.) to allow for fresh spontaneity in each film. How Felix accomplishes his goal is more important than the goal itself.

Felix's endlessly inventive and magical solutions to problems is affected by his well-known personality, which is a major source of delight and laughter to audiences. But sometimes the design of certain scenes surprises the eye with its elegant, simple beauty; for example, the breathtaking chiaroscuro effect in *Sure-Locked Homes* (April 15) when silhouetted Felix passes a window and his shadow is thrown across a moonlit room.

As effective and popular as the Felix films were in the fall of 1928, change was in the air since Disney's success with sound made him the talk of the animation industry. His Mickey Mouse was an overnight star, as Felix had been nearly ten years earlier.

Mickey resembled Felix in other ways: both shared the same round shapes for body and head, the same black coloring and white face mask, but Mickey's ears were large and round instead of small and pointed. Veteran Disney animator Ollie Johnston defends Disney's design choice, noting that "the shapes and markings of Felix and Mickey,

A film frame from *Sure-Locked Homes* (1928). Courtesy Donald Crafton.

perhaps more than Oswald [the Lucky Rabbit], have similarities, but when you are using such simple basic construction [i.e., circles] there is bound to be some duplication." Animator Frank Thomas, who along with Johnston was one of Disney's finest "personality" animators, concurs: ". . . they [early studio animators] all drew pointed ears on cats, round ears on mice and a double lump for an ear on a bulldog; that was standard design throughout the industry." He explains, "Walt had too much ego and too much curiosity to ever copy anyone else in the first place. His philosophy of 'What can we do with it?' assumed that anything could be made better with a little work."

What needed work was Mickey Mouse's personality; in his first film, he has none. Nor did Mickey have Felix's near decade's worth of audience familiarity and affection going for him. In *Steamboat Willie*, Mickey displays a mindless sadism that is interesting only because of the synchronized music and sounds it forces from a variety of unlucky animals; by various tortures—pulling a cat's tail, strumming a goose's neck, tweaking a sow's teats, twisting a goat's tail, and so on—"Turkey in the Straw" is rendered.

Felix the Cat, on the other hand, was "a very inventive personality," says Ollie Johnston, "meaning that his creators had endowed him with an exceedingly resourceful and agile mind. To me he was an entertaining personality who was full of surprises. I don't remember any of the other early characters, Farmer Al Falfa or Aesop's Fables, impressing me in the same way. . . . Felix was the first character that had a personality and I'm sure that didn't go unnoticed by Walt."

The only comment Frank Thomas ever heard Walt Disney make about Felix the Cat was in regard to personality animation: "They have little bits of personality here and there on Felix, but they don't go near far enough." Disney eventually developed a unique personality for Mickey Mouse that was universally appealing, and sound helped him do it. Sound tracks offered a new dynamic to dimensionalize a character's personality and tone down the exaggerated pantomime gestures used in silent cartoons. With sound came the use of stronger storytelling pose drawings to emphasize dialogue or accent musical beats; drawings became more subtle and expressive using the pose method.

Disney was to move his cartoons far away from the two-dimensional,

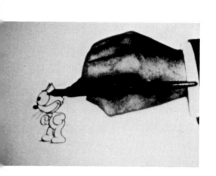

A film frame from
Comicalamities (1928).
Courtesy Donald Crafton.

irrational world in which Felix the Cat was king, and aim toward naturalism and a caricature of life forces using sound, color, weight, and fluid motion. For Felix to make similar changes would be to destroy what made him Felix: a perfect adaptation of the limitations of the silent animation medium and an icon of the period in which he thrived.

There was pressure for Pat Sullivan to change his films to sound. His distributor, Educational Pictures, wanted Felix to talk, but Sullivan, his judgment blurred by alcohol, hesitated. Why change? was his attitude. For a decade, Sullivan had relied on the creative efforts of others and removed himself completely from the filmmaking process; now he was deeply insecure as to how to meet the technological challenge sound presented.

Educational did not renew their contract with Sullivan after the 1928–1929 series. Staff layoffs followed at the studio and included Hal Walker, who had been there since 1920. "I'll never forget the total frustration that I had of dejection of being fired," said Walker. "When I told [my wife] Gladys, it was like the world came to an end. I was eating, breathing, sleeping Felix the Cat. It was a very difficult thing for me to recondition myself to think beyond my immediate chaotic condition." Messmer, of course, stayed on and a skeleton crew of freelancers were hired as needed.

Sullivan finally decided to add sound to completed Felix cartoons, some old, some new, and he made a deal with former Bray studio manager-turned-producer Jacques Kopfstein, who distributed them through Copley Pictures Corporation. An ad in the October 16, 1929, *Film Daily* shows Felix announcing, Jolson-like, "You ain't heard nothin' yet!"

Unfortunately, audiences heard nothin' good from Sullivan's excursion into sound. All of the music and sound effects for Felix were postsynchronized; that is, the sound tracks were recorded after the picture was finished. Disney did the opposite: he carefully prepared his tracks first by analyzing them frame by frame, and then animated action to match the track, resulting in a perfect wedding of image and sound. Felix's tracks, with Bernard Altshuler's Symphonic Recording Orchestra and Harry Edison's sound effects, were sloppy, rarely matching the action on the screen. Music and effects were also unimaginatively produced; Felix's "voice," for example, became an annoying whine.

Hal Walker put it succinctly: "By 1930 Felix was doomed because he was a silent pantomime character. We tried sound but it was a flop."

By 1930, Mickey Mouse was a national sensation, and Disney's *Silly Symphonies* series (begun in 1929) brought the creative merging of track and picture to new heights, which led within a decade to a sound-and-image achievement titled *Fantasia* (1940).

On January 23 and March 8, 1930, Sullivan placed notices in the trade journal *Motion Picture News*, claiming he was in Hollywood producing three Felix sound cartoons for independent release and planned to move his staff from New York to Los Angeles. He also announced the closing of a deal with Technicolor and Harriscolor for "the exclusive use of each process for animated color cartoons over a term of years."

Messmer never made films outside New York and Sullivan never produced color films with or without Felix. The two trade articles were desperate attempts to stem the tide of overwhelming indifference the industry and the public were showing toward Sullivan and his once popular cartoon star.

One of Sullivan's last interviews, published in December 1930, was granted to a couple of cartoon fans writing for an obscure periodical, *The Commerce Caravel.* The article is a textbook example of a faded celebrity attempting to put on a smooth show of confidence for what remains of his public.

The two writers "haunted" Sullivan's studio for four days before finding the producer in, and, noticing a lack of activity in the place, naively asked, "Is Felix working on any picture now?"

"Of course he is," Sullivan replied. "Mr. Thurber—our photographer—is even now in the midst of one. We have arranged no title as yet."

Sullivan seemed pleased by the attention of the two writers and their fanzine questions. He easily deflected potentially troublesome inquiries, such as "How do you get your ideas?" (Answer: "By being curious like you are"), preferring to hold forth with his oft-repeated story of Felix's origin ("I received the idea of putting Felix on paper from my wife"), and his gracious admiration for fellow cartoonists ("among them, of course, Walter Disney with his inimitable Mickey Mouse . . . an excellent character [who] certainly deserves every bit of his present popularity").

Sometimes Sullivan expressed his own feelings through Felix: "Just today, [Felix] received an enthusiastic letter from a great fan of his in Japan. Was he glad to get it? You bet he was." Was Sullivan glad to get it? You bet he was.

Sullivan, in marked contrast to his descriptions of the character as a Frankenstein monster five years earlier in London, expressed an unusual affection for Felix: "Felix sees to it that I work, and I love him." At the end of the interview, Sullivan stated, "No, I have no children," then reconsidered. "Yes, I have. Felix is both child and friend to me."

In the interview, Sullivan mentioned the completion of only a few new film titles, which indicates Felix's formerly full production schedule was now sporadic. "Three weeks ago," he said, "[Felix] completed *Skulls and Sculls*—a college sport picture. A week ago he finished *April Maze*, in which he has one jolly time at a picnic, and a few weeks before that he put out *Hootchy Kootchy Parlais Vous*, a war picture in which Felix is at his best."

April Maze exemplifies the creative dilemma placed on Messmer, who attempted to make sound films that could compete with Disney but was saddled with the postsync method. The film's opening scene resembles a Silly Symphony as a butterfly (animated with large floppy wings) bounces interminably from flower to flower. Next, the flowers dance in a repeated cycle before their petals form hands and they applaud themselves. This "overture" seems to say, "Look, I'm a sound cartoon, just like Disney"; unfortunately it also calls attention to the on-again, off-again synchronization, and worse, it delays the appearance of Felix. He and two kittens eventually show up and try to enjoy a picnic in the woods, which is constantly interrupted by rain and various hungry animals. In *April Maze*, a now thoroughly domesticated Felix seems to have lost his edge. In the role as a good daddy, he is boring, lacks zest and his old magical resourcefulness; metamorphosis is used sparingly without the pleasing surprises of years past. Supporting char-

Four film frames from *Oceantics* (1930). Courtesy Donald Crafton.

acters (a rabbit, snake, bear, and stork) dominate the screen footage; the film meanders and has a lost and exhausted quality to it.

What a contrast to *Felix the Cat Woos Whoopee*, one of the best Felix films ever made. The short has been dated 1928 as well as 1930; prints available today have postsynced sound. If it is from the former date, *Woos Whoopee* is an example of Messmer's lively direction in his prime; if the latter date, it can be seen as a last hurrah, a final burst of vibrant creative energy.

The film opens in a neon-lit metropolis, where even the buildings bounce to a jazz beat. Felix is the life of the party at the Whoopee Club—drinking, throwing confetti, blowing horns, dancing—he is the epitome of motion, rhythm, and life. Cut to Felix's home, where his angry wife, rolling pin in hand, paces the floor in measured steps and watches the clock.

When Felix leaves the club in the wee hours of the morning, his intoxicated state induces hallucinations. The streets beneath his staggering feet heave and weave wildly, an effeminate lamppost becomes a fire-breathing dragon and chases him, as does a monstrous elephant-turned-ape with wings. A snake turns into a jalopy, in which Felix speedily escapes. But his delirium tremens intensifies and he falls through space, gets swallowed by a fish/sax/trumpet that finally chases him home. It is 6:00 A.M. when he puts his tail in an umbrella stand and removes his furry "shoes" to stealthily tiptoe up stairs resembling soft piano keys. Felix almost escapes his wife's wrath, until a final hallucination makes him attack a pillow he mistakes for a mocking chicken. The Mrs. awakens and kicks her philandering husband out.

Woos Whoopee contrasts responsible behavior with irresponsibility, controlled movement with uncontrollable energy, the restrictions of domesticity with the pleasures of freedom, sobriety with ecstasy.

By 1931, it was over for Felix. The dizzying heights of celebrity proved treacherous and slippery, the public incredibly fickle. Felix, the cat, who brought good fortune to others both on the screen and off, had run out of luck himself. He was no longer a film star, no longer even appearing in films. Felix merchandising began to dry up. Felix was old hat; Mickey Mouse was the new king of cartoons and character licensing.

Sullivan, with no other characters or plans for new animated films, was suddenly as much of a has-been as Felix. Their careers were so closely tied together that Felix brought Sullivan down with him. Sullivan's oft-expressed fear of Felix's stranglehold on him was now a reality. Contemplating the sudden demise of his and Felix the Cat's career must have sunk Sullivan into an alcoholic depression the depths of which can only be imagined.

Two film frames from *Felix the Cat Woos Whoopee* (1928 or 1930). Courtesy Donald Crafton.

Then, on Saturday, March 26, 1932, Marjorie Sullivan leaned out the window of her apartment on the second floor of the Forrest Hotel on Forty-ninth Street. According to her death certificate, Mrs. Sullivan "fell or jumped from residence to ground" headfirst. Four days later, she was buried.

There were those, like Hal Walker and Harry Kopp's daughters, who thought Marjorie's death was a suicide. But others, including Otto Messmer, felt Marjorie loved life too much to commit suicide and thought her death was accidental. In a small obituary on March 27, the *New York Times* reported that, according to detectives, Marjorie was merely attempting "to attract the attention of her chauffeur," who was in her Cadillac at a garage across the street, when she lost her balance.

Marjorie Sullivan "never jumped," said her niece, Betty Jean Buckley. "She had everything." Certainly Marjorie did not lack for money: she left, at the beginnings of the Depression, an estate of upwards of $70,000, including forty-three railroad and industrial bonds and a first mortgage certificate amounting to $43,000; the estate was exclusive of a claim against the Bank of United States in liquidation, where at the time of its closing she had on deposit about $79,000.

There is little information about the relationship between Pat and Marjorie Sullivan. Marjorie's niece was a child when the couple made

133

occasional visits to Scranton and remembers Uncle Pat and Aunt Marjorie as "a great couple. Down to earth, easy-going and friendly."

But a number of adults saw the Sullivans in a different light. Mrs. Otto Messmer remembered "they had plenty of battles. Battling all the time. Miserable life. With all their money it didn't give them happiness." George Winkler, brother of Sullivan's first distributor, recalls Pat and Marjorie were together "very little. He wasn't with her very much." Hal Walker goes further: "Pat was an alcoholic and a sex maniac. He was taking some of his money and financed a madam, put her in business in one of the famous hotels in New York City and had quite a stable of females. It was quite natural the outcome of this that he developed a very bad case of syphilis, which he then gave to his wife, Marjorie. On that trip to England, it erupted so badly on her body, she had to wear specially designed scarves to cover . . . her face and neck. . . . They lived in the name of man and wife. I know personally he used Marjorie for purposes of influencing other men, which was a great discredit to Pat in my eyes. I just couldn't believe such men existed."

In the early part of 1932, Sullivan's health rapidly failed, and after the death of his wife he became not only more physically disabled but also showed traits of mental disorder. Whether caused by grief over Marjorie's death, years of alcohol abuse, or the tertiary stage of syphilis that finally affects the brain, or a combination of all three, it was obvious that Pat Sullivan was losing his mind. "This mental condition," related Kopp, "took expression in spending money lavishly on women and issuing a great number of checks without any consideration, a large number of which were returned for insufficient funds. . . ."

By the end of 1932, Sullivan's memory began to fade. He didn't recognize Otto Messmer, who continued to draw the Sunday Felix comic strip. Worse, Messmer couldn't cash his checks because Sullivan's handwriting had deteriorated into a scrawl.

Pat Sullivan died in Sherman Square Hospital on February 15, 1933, at 9:15 A.M. of "chronic alcoholism" and "terminal lobular pneumonia." He was forty-eight years old.

In November, Felix the Cat made his first appearance in the ninth annual Macy's Thanksgiving Day Parade. During that terrible Depression year, the sight of a smiling Felix balloon trundling on wheels down Broadway must have been bittersweet to onlookers, a nostalgic reminder (practically a ghost) of better, more prosperous times. It was also a symbolic indication that, though separated from both of his masters (through Sullivan's death and Messmer's disinterest), the Cat would come back.

A Felix balloon in the 1933 Macy's Thanksgiving Day Parade. Courtesy Macy's.

COMEBACK

9

AFTER SULLIVAN'S DEATH, his lawyer Harry Kopp tried to straighten out Sullivan's tangled affairs. A search was made at the copyright office in Washington, D.C., and Kopp discovered that the Felix comic strip was registered by King Features on May 7, 1929, but the registration had never been assigned to Sullivan. "Like-wise, the record revealed," said Kopp, "that the deceased never retained any property right in the comic strips, which had been published by the Syndicate for many years past, which, of course, gave the Syndicate the right to republish these strips at any time. These registrations not only raised a serious question of law as to whether the deceased had any rights in the Felix comic strip, but also it made it absolutely impossible to get any other Syndicate to bid for it."

Further, Kopp was amazed to find that Sullivan was "an employee" of the Syndicate, not "an independent artist owning the copyright to the strip he was making."

The contract was to expire in 1934, so Kopp began six months of negotiations with King Features to continue the publication of the Felix strip, which "was of importance to the estate for the reason that the popularity of the subject depended exclusively upon such continuous publication." Since Felix no longer had a movie career, his visibility in newspapers was necessary for the estate to continue licensing Felix's image on merchandise and receive royalties.

On February 25, Kopp received a letter from Otto Messmer, saying "he had been promised by Mr. Sullivan that the copyright to Felix, as well as the trademark, would be left to him upon his death and while

Opposite: Joe Oriolo in 1976. Collection of the author.

he did not make any particular legal claim to it, he threatened to take a position with Walt Disney in California or elsewhere unless an immediate adjustment was made with the King Features Syndicate, Inc., whereby he could continue to draw this cartoon as before." Messmer also filed a claim against the Sullivan estate for "two weeks' wages" owed him, amounting to $400.

The King Features attorneys took the position that the copyright was the property of the syndicate and if Kopp insisted upon raising any question as to that right, "they were quite content to discontinue the publication of the strips altogether." After numerous conferences between Kopp, lawyers for the Sullivan heirs in Australia, and King Features, the syndicate agreed to pay the estate $2,000 for its right, title, and interest, if any, to the copyright. King Features also agreed to release to the estate whatever rights it had to the "Felix" trademark or to the retention of any royalties for the use of the name "Felix," and to abstain from making any contracts for the use of the character Felix the Cat other than the publication of the comic strip.

Kopp also discovered "most of the royalties collected by the deceased prior to his death were under oral arrangements which I knew nothing of until I commenced to receive checks as executor of the estate." There were also a number of copyright infringements of the trademark "which had to be protected so that these royalties might continue to flow into the estate."

One infringement was a proposed Felix design used as a wall clock; the item—a Felix look-alike with moving eyes and pendulum tail—is sold to this day because Kopp investigated and concluded the matter was not of sufficient importance to warrant the expenditure of a large sum of money contesting the originator's application for a patent.

In March, Kopp fought a packing company in Los Angeles that applied to the U.S. Patent Office for use of the name "Felix," and he terminated a contract with the Cameo Doll Company when he found "it had not paid any royalties for many years." He learned through Messmer that the American Lead Pencil Company was extensively advertising pencils and packing them in boxes with drawings of the trademark character made by Messmer, "operating under an oral agreement which they made with Sullivan for a royalty based on a percentage basis." Kopp allowed the oral agreement to continue until a later one in writing could be entered upon.

George Borgfeldt and Company had a contract with Sullivan for the distribution of Felix dolls and novelties; as with King Features, the trademark for Felix dolls and toys had been taken out by Borgfeldt and Company, but had never been assigned by them to Sullivan. However, Kopp concluded, "The matter was not of such great importance as the royalties from that source had dropped to almost a vanishing point." Since 1930, Borgfeldt had been manufacturing and selling Mickey Mouse dolls and toys, which eclipsed Felix in popularity and profitability.

Kopp attempted to negotiate a contract for the production and distribution of new Felix animated cartoons on a percentage basis in order to yield a profit to the estate. He negotiated with Patrick A. Powers, a notoriously unscrupulous independent producer. Powers once battled Carl Laemmle for control of Universal (tossing the corporate ledgers out a window to avoid examination) and he owned the sound system Walt Disney used to record the track for *Steamboat Willie*. Powers distributed Mickey Mouse films from late 1928 to early 1930 until the Disney brothers discovered, as Roy Disney put it, "That guy's a crook."

Kopp found Powers "willing to distribute the pictures on a percentage basis," but the wily producer had no intention of risking his money with the formerly popular Felix. He insisted that the estate pay the initial cost of the production, which amounted to about $7,000 or $8,000 per film, a proposition Kopp advised the legatees "would be an unprofitable arrangement, which they should not go into."

For the rest of his life, Otto Messmer blamed Harry Kopp rather than his own passivity for his permanent disconnection with Felix the Cat: "His lawyer just closed the studio, you know? I had no authority being a salaried man under [Sullivan] and I didn't own any part of [Felix]. I couldn't start a new contract, you see, I coulda finished an old one, but anyway . . ."

Messmer, known in the animation industry as the creative power behind Felix all those years, always claimed, "The minute Sullivan died MGM [and] RKO called me up immediately. They thought I was part owner of it. They said we'll pay for the studio, we'll open it up

139

for you. Please come. They wanted to get behind Felix in color with a big staff. . . . At that time, I was hangin' on to the pages and the strips. . . . But this Kopp tried to contact Sullivan's survivors over in Australia. For some reason or other they took a helluva long time to come over. By that time things changed a little bit. So I kinda forgot all about Felix. . . ."

Kopp, a meticulous lawyer who preferred to take care of every detail in a case himself, had his hands full dealing with Sullivan's brother and father. First he had to locate them; then he had to communicate with them halfway around the world through two law firms hired by each of the Sullivans. There was also "some conflict of interest between the legatees," a difference of opinion regarding the estate that caused the feuding father and son to change law firms twice. As of July 1934, Pat Sullivan's net cash estate was $34,605.82.

One day in 1935, the head of the Van Beuren studio called Messmer in for an interview. Amedee Van Beuren had made his fortune selling peep-show mutoscopes, and formed his own animation studio in 1928 after seven years producing Paul Terry's *Aesop's Fables*.

The mustachioed producer told Messmer he was frustrated by his staff's inability to create popular cartoon characters. Tom and Jerry (a human team, not the famous cat and mouse team that MGM produced years later) and Cubby Bear were bland and failed to interest the public. Van Beuren, who in desperation once copied the design of Mickey and Minnie Mouse so closely Walt Disney sued for copyright infringement, also used established characters for his films. A series based on Otto Soglow's comic strip *The Little King* and an adaptation from radio's *Amos 'n' Andy* both failed.

In 1934, he hired Burt Gillett away from the Disney studio. Gillett (who had worked with Messmer at the Sullivan studio for seven years) was well known in the animation industry as the director of Disney's *Three Little Pigs*, and Van Beuren offered him a princely salary. But the characters Gillett created for Van Beuren—Molly Moo Cow and the feathery cast from Parrotville—proved not to be star material either.

Now Van Beuren thought of Felix the Cat, who had been off movie screens for nearly five years and whose main public exposure was the

comic strip Messmer continued to draw. "Van Beuren called me up," said Messmer. "Didn't care what salary I would mention, he'd give [it to] me to save his place because . . . there was great discontent . . . cause he didn't have any characters, they were all trying to make up something. . . . At this time, I started getting a little interested because he was so persistent."

A comeback opportunity for both Felix and Messmer had fallen miraculously into Messmer's lap. With Van Beuren's financial backing, studio staff, and technology, Messmer would be free from business details and could concentrate on creating and directing the films, as he had under Pat Sullivan. Here was a chance for Messmer to modernize Felix with sound and three-toned Technicolor and perhaps challenge Disney's supremacy. Was this not the answer to Messmer's hopes?

Apparently not, for he hesitated and wriggled out of a commitment, telling Van Beuren he needed to go to the hospital for a sinus operation. Messmer, who was basically a loner and an idea man, may have wearied at the thought of again directing a staff of cartoonists; after years of leading other artists, he may have preferred the insularity and directness involved in making comic strips. He may also have felt insecure about his ability to make cartoons in the new technology of sound and color, and feared failure. Whatever the reason, Messmer allowed his last opportunity to direct and animate Felix the Cat in a series of films to pass easily. He sealed his fate by recommending Burt Gillett. "After I get out of the hospital in a month I may join," he told Van Beuren. "You can get the Felix rights from the estate."

Van Beuren received permission from the Sullivan estate to produce three Felix cartoons and assigned them to Gillett to direct. When Messmer finally did express interest in working on the new Felix films, Gillett bluntly told him his approach was old-fashioned and out of step with "modern" cartoons: "He figured my style with the old silent Felix wouldn't fit."

Years later, Messmer regretted suggesting Gillett for the job: "The worst thing I could ever have done was to recommend him." Gillett's success "out there" in Hollywood, thought Messmer, "went to his head. The ego was in him now."

Gillett was no doubt an egotist, but he was also manic-depressive, with violent mood swings and irrational behavior that resulted in turmoil at the Van Beuren studio. He attempted to run the place like Disney's, shifting personnel around, firing them, hiring replacements, and instituting new procedures—such as shooting animation "pencil tests" in order to make motion changes before final color. But improvements in the mechanics of animation came with a high price tag, as did Gillett's indecision and constant staff firings.

Out of this backstage turmoil came *Felix the Cat and the Goose That Laid the Golden Eggs* (released February 7, 1936), *Neptune Nonsense* (March 20), and *Bold King Cole* (May 29), all part of Van Beuren's Rainbow Parade series of Technicolor shorts. In the films, Felix start-

A film frame from *Neptune Nonsense* (1936). Courtesy UCLA Film Archives/Jerry Guldin/David Shepard.

lingly resembles Mickey Mouse in looks, high-pitched voice, and boyish personality. The comparison with Disney's films is enhanced by Winston Shaples's bright and tuneful musical direction (arranged for full orchestra) that follows the action exactly and cleverly comments on it. Van Beuren's generous budgets show up on the screen, which is busy with a multitude of characters performing fully animated actions and lavish special effects, such as storms, sea waves, underwater ripples, and translucent ghosts.

In *Goose That Laid the Golden Eggs*, Gillett uses a few visual bits from the silent Messmer films, e.g., Felix's walk while thinking, certain sad or concerned facial expressions, and detaching his tail for use as a fuse for a cannon and turning himself into the cannonball. The director obviously felt it necessary to connect his constantly moving slick Mickey look-alike with the old staccato inkblot Felix of yore—if only to remind audiences who his character is supposed to be. There is a grudging feeling in the use of the old metamorphic bits, and they considerably diminish in use in the last two shorts. In *Neptune Nonsense*, for example, Felix's tail detaches from his rear to become an exclamation point, but the action is so poorly staged and brief it is difficult to see.

Years later Leonard Maltin criticized the Felix cannonball scene in *Goose* this way:

What could have been a rousing turning point in the film and conferred a mark of individuality on an otherwise Mickey Mouse–like character, becomes instead a throwaway as directed by Gillett. . . . The gag is played without fanfare, in long shot, against a highly colored backdrop, and a wonderful opportunity is lost. This film, along with *Neptune's Nonsense*, and especially *Bold King Cole*, have ingenious story elements that could have been wrought into great cartoons, but as they now stand, the parts are greater than the whole, and the least interesting factor is the personality of Felix.

Less certainly proved to be more when animating Felix the Cat. The silent Messmer-directed films remind one of haiku, the Japanese verse-form emotional statements about the seasons, which must be composed

143

within three lines containing only seventeen syllables. Change one structural or thematic element and it is no longer haiku. So it was with Felix: sound, color, full animation, a cast of hundreds, and Disney-like illusory special effects diminished rather than enhanced his essence. The limited technology of the silent cartoons, Messmer's special genius, and the elegant simplicity of Felix were a perfect combination. Change one of those elements and you no longer had Felix.

"Felix was just a little figure in the background, instead of being the center figure," said Messmer in a gentle criticism of Gillett's version of Felix. "He tried to push his own characters in there. Gillett tried to push himself, rather than the Cat."

Gillett had planned a fourth film, *Felix Among the Royalty*, in which Felix goes to heaven and "meets all the ancient kings and queens." When the Cat tells Saint Peter that on earth he was a movie star, "Peter sends him to hell, where he's happy in the company of other actors." The idea never got beyond a three-page typed treatment, for Van Beuren lost his distribution deal when RKO signed Walt Disney in 1936. The studio closed and Van Beuren died one year later of a heart attack at age fifty-eight. Burt Gillett bounced unhappily from studio to studio (even making a brief return to Disney's).

Otto Messmer continued to draw the Sunday Felix comic strips until their discontinuance in 1943, when he began eleven years of writing and drawing monthly Felix comic books for Dell Publishing; the daily Felix newspaper strip continued until 1967.

From March 1944 to December 1945, Messmer worked at Famous Studios (the former Fleischer studio) on storyboards for films starring Popeye and Little Lulu. A letter from Sam Buchwald, president of Famous, to Messmer dated April 3, 1946, mentions the completion of two shorts "you worked on, namely the underwater picture with Popeye PEEP IN THE DEEP and OLD MACDONALD. They turned out nicely with good reactions from all corners." Buchwald offers to purchase new film ideas "should you ever have any spare time" and notes, "It does seem a shame that we are unable to have your excellent talents for our company."

The reason Messmer was not available for full-time employment at Famous or other animation studios was because for the remainder of

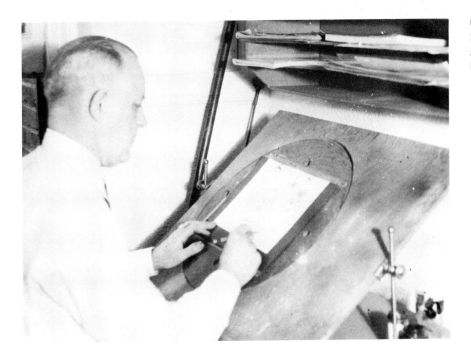

his career, from 1937 until he retired in 1973, he worked for Douglas Leigh, the "Sign King" or "Lamplighter of Broadway." It was Leigh who for years produced what he described as "spectaculars"; that is, "an oversized advertising display with neons or lamps in unusual animations."

Leigh was master of the mammoth electric signs (some covering more than 1,000 square feet) that lit up Times Square and similar urban spaces around the world. Walter Winchell once described Leigh's signs as the Disney technique of animation transferred to lights. In 1937, a display called the Leigh-EPOK Spectacular was brought to life by the Messmer technique of animation.

Leigh hired a number of animators to create moving graphics for the EPOK spectaculars, including former Disney hand Hutch Hutchinson and Norman McLaren, who later founded the animation division at the National Film Board of Canada. But Leigh's "chief animator" was, of course, Otto Messmer.

It must be considered something of a miracle that this particular job should find its way to Messmer, for he and EPOK were obviously a

145

Messmer (left) discusses with Douglas Leigh a storyboard for a giant animated electric sign. Courtesy Doris Messmer.

perfect match. Here was work incredibly similar to what Messmer did when he first joined Pat Sullivan's studio nearly a quarter of a century before: thinking up silent visual gags for black-silhouetted characters. Also, as at Sullivan's from 1916 to 1920, Messmer could work alone, seeing single films through to completion with only a blackener to fill in his drawn outlines.

Messmer was once again shielded from bothersome business details by a strong entrepreneur, who paid him a steady weekly salary for anonymously creating lively cartoon characters that would be seen by a worldwide audience. In 1937, while Walt Disney's bold developments

146

in sound, color, motion, and storytelling and personality animation led the animation industry toward new and unprecedented technological and narrative heights—as exemplified by the premiere of his first feature-length animated film, *Snow White and the Seven Dwarfs*— Messmer was happily cocooned in an animation time warp.

Messmer's full-time day schedule at Leigh's necessitated his working on the monthly Felix comic book and daily strips at night. Finally, he sought help and approached two ex-Famous Studio animators, Jim Tyer and Joe Oriolo.

"Otto started falling behind, he had to turn out so many pages," said Oriolo. Tyer soon dropped out, leaving Oriolo and Messmer to share the comic-book cartooning chores: "Messmer did part of the book and I did part of the book." As time went by, Oriolo, an inventive cartoonist with a robust style, assumed most of the responsibility for illustrating the Felix comics. Within a few years, Oriolo would assume responsibility for everything to do with Felix and would, literally, own the character. Oriolo's energy, determination, and entrepreneurial instincts would once again make Felix the Cat a viable and valuable commercial commodity.

An advertisement for Mattel Toys, drawn by Otto Messmer, one of many clients using Leigh-EPOK animated electric signs. Courtesy Doris Messmer.

In April 1933, at age twenty, Oriolo had started as an errand boy at the Max Fleischer Studio, but his obvious talent as a draftsman and his ambition advanced him to the position of animator within one year. Oriolo was part of director Dave Tendlar's crew animating on Betty Boop shorts (e.g., *A Song for a Day*, 1936), Popeye shorts (e.g., *I Wanna Be a Lifeguard*, 1936), and Color Classics, such as *The Cobweb Hotel* (1936), although he did not receive screen credit until *Tears of an Onion* in 1938.

Joe Oriolo enjoyed the rough-and-tumble atmosphere of the Fleischer studio and when it moved to Miami in 1938, he went with it. He worked with a number of directors, including Al Eugster, former Sullivan studio blackener, now a veteran of Disney's and a Fleischer "head animator," on *A Hull of a Mess* (1942), and Myron Waldman on *Raggedy Ann and Andy* (1941). Oriolo animated on both of the Fleischer features, *Gulliver's Travels* (1939), in which he also provided the voice of an Italian barber, and *Mr. Bug Goes to Town* (1941).

Paramount took over the Fleischer studio in 1942 and reestablished it in New York as Famous Studios. Oriolo left Famous in 1944 to freelance animating on armed forces/industrial films, as well as some of the earliest TV commercials, and drawing comic books, such as Fawcett's *George Pal Puppetoons*. He also gained experience as an entrepreneur-producer by farming out animation scenes to moonlighting Famous Studios personnel and serving as a middleman between comic-book publishers and cartoonists. In the midforties, Messmer sought Oriolo's help on the Felix comics, and little by little the older man gave the energetic younger cartoonist more and more pages to fill.

Pat Sullivan, son of the now deceased W. J. O'Sullivan and namesake nephew of the famous and long deceased Pat Sullivan, arrived in New York from Australia in the summer of 1950. In May, Felix the Cat Productions, Inc., succeeded Felix the Cat, Inc., and in October, young Sullivan attended a meeting of the directors of Felix the Cat Productions, Inc., who included E. W. Poindexter and Otto Messmer.

Sometime in 1953, Joe Oriolo heard that King Features Syndicate

Messmer at his desk at Douglas Leigh Organization. Courtesy Doris Messmer.

"was going to take the [comic] strip away from Messmer, and they called me in. But I wouldn't take it. I said, 'Look, it's his character. Why the hell should I take it?' So they let him do it again for a whole year."

It was not the first time King Features attempted to replace Messmer. In a December 5, 1941, letter to Messmer, W. J. O'Sullivan wrote: "I was very disappointed when I found out that King Features had asked another artist to do Felix for a time. I wrote to Mr. Poindexter about the position and was very relieved when he was able to tell me that you were again back at work."

Through the years, Messmer received numerous memos from King Features executives informing him of changes in page layouts and format sizes, but also often criticizing his work. "Mr. [J. V.] Connelly thinks your daily strips are strung out a little thin," Bradley Kelly wrote to Messmer on April 21, 1942. "Perhaps you can get a more compact gag in each strip."

The most ominous memo to Messmer, dated April 2, 1954, from one Sylvan Byck of King Features, was instigated by young Pat Sullivan, who "has been quite disturbed because FELIX [the comic strip] is not more successful."

At age sixty-two, Messmer had drawn Felix strips for over three decades. A certain amount of repetition, as was to be expected, crept in, and to begin with, the strip was never wildly popular. Sullivan's heir, wishing to maximize the economic potential of his legacy, sought a reason for Felix's current lackluster career. Messmer became an unresisting scapegoat and King Features willingly played hatchet man.

Joe Oriolo remembered that in 1954 King Features was going to drop Messmer again and was seeking other cartoonists to fill his shoes. "[King] asked me to do a couple of weeks [of strips] and I did and they wanted me to continue it. So I did it for about fifteen years after that. But I never felt right about it. I always felt it wasn't my character."

He always admired Otto Messmer as "one of the best creative guys I've ever seen. He can make something out of nothing." But Oriolo also knew of the opportunities to own and control Felix that Messmer passed up. "He really is a broken-hearted guy within himself, only he doesn't show it. Messmer is the type of guy who works his heart out

and when he does something he really puts his mind to it. But he's a
dreamer. He'll talk about the past, he'll talk nostalgia.

"If Otto had done what he should have done and continued on, he
could have been bigger than Disney today."

Oriolo saw possibilities in Felix—mainly a comeback in animation
and merchandising—that Messmer did not. He took steps to protect
himself, as Messmer had not, by gradually assuming legal ownership
of the character. Felix the Cat Creations was incorporated in 1958 as
a wholly owned subsidiary of Felix the Cat Productions, Inc., to produce
films, with Joe Oriolo and Pat Sullivan as two of the four directors.
The subsidiary was dissolved in 1971 and Oriolo became a director
and eventually, after Pat Sullivan's death, president of Felix the Cat
Productions, Inc.

Reviving Felix was not easy. Most of the film and TV corporations
Oriolo and Sullivan approached considered the character old-hat, if not
moribund. Trans-Lux became interested only after Oriolo put up his
own money to finance a pilot for a TV series. On the strength of Oriolo's
film, $1,750,000 in sales was appropriated to produce 260 *Felix* epi-
sodes. The format could run as four-minute individual episodes or a
continuing quarter hour, thus providing programming flexibility to
stations.

By February 1959, Oriolo was deep into production with his directors, most of them former Fleischer head animators, including Jim Tyer,
Steve Muffati, Frank Endres, Rube Grossman, Tom Johnson, George
Rufle, Red Auguston, George Germanetti, and Al Eugster. The staff
was well paid, the studio well equipped with modern equipment, but
the amount of footage required (one animator was pushing out 150 feet
a week) was enormous and the pace grueling.

Oriolo was also trying to educate his staff of middle-aged former
Fleischer animators in the new style of "limited" TV animation per-
fected by Hanna-Barbera. One of his dictums became well known
within the industry: scenes that could not fit under his office door, said
Oriolo, held too many drawings. Such fully animated scenes were considered a threat to the budget and were sent back to the animator for
changes.

Oriolo's *Felix* series is remembered fondly by first-generation tele-

vision viewers. In it, a redesigned long-legged Felix participates in lightly humorous adventures with a supporting cast consisting of the gruff bulldog Rock Bottom, the mad Professor, and his overly bright nephew Poindexter (named after Oriolo's lawyer). Metamorphosis was rarely used, but, in a bow to Felix's past association with magical transformations, Felix carried a "Magic Bag," a valise that changed into sundry objects and protected him from harm. A third song was composed for the Cat, which opened and closed each show:

> Felix the Cat. The wonderful, wonderful Cat.
> You'll laugh so hard your sides will ache, your heart
> will go pitter-pat . . . watching Felix the wonderful Cat!

The *Felix* TV series proved successful and a second one was planned, but Trans-Lux refused to come up with the money to support such a large studio and Oriolo was forced to disband.

Oriolo went on to produce an action series for TV (*The Mighty Hercules*) and to import foreign series, as well as produce TV commercials. The animated *Felix* series continued to play on television around the globe. In 1982, Felix the Cat Productions produced fifty-two live-action half-hour TV programs in color featuring Felix; a full-page ad in the March 10, 1982, *Variety* described the series: "Felix the timeless and ageless feline, travels the gamut from submarines to space stations, showing children how to laugh and learn at the same time."

Much of Joe Oriolo's time, up until his death on Christmas Day, 1985, was occupied with overseeing the merchandising of Felix the Cat. Thanks to the high visibility of the *Felix* TV series, both animated and live-action, a variety of manufacturers became interested—for the first time since the 1920s—in licensing Felix's image. Cannon Mills, for example, printed Felix on bedding and linen and Don Kreiss, Inc., made plush Felix slippers. Determined Productions began marketing Felix bags, toys, T-shirts, coffee mugs, greeting cards, and plush Felix dolls. In 1984, Felix co-starred with Betty Boop in a short-lived comic strip drawn by the Walker Brothers (sons of cartoonist Mort Walker).

The revival of interest in Felix led to curiosity about the history of the character, and Oriolo was always careful in interviews to credit

Messmer. "Sunday, May 18th," he told an interviewer in 1975, "when we had the retrospective in Washington [D.C., as part of the American Film Institute's Second Anniversary in the Kennedy Center], I made it a point to bring out the fact that Messmer was the one who really created Felix the Cat and not Pat Sullivan." Oriolo gave credit to Messmer around the world, including licensing meetings in Japan and Singapore, and a 1978 Felix the Cat film retrospective at the Zagreb (Yugoslavia) International Animation Festival.

But Oriolo also made clear his thoughts about the significance of his contribution to the revival of interest in the famous character and his place in the history of animation. "The whole trouble is," he said, "since I took Felix, all due respect to Messmer and Pat Sullivan, really, I'm the guy, Joe Oriolo is the guy who really kept this thing goin'.

"But one thing about Otto Messmer: he is an unsung hero and he'll go down in the history of animation. . . . And I hope that I get recognition on Felix in the future like he has been gettin' through me. I hope somebody has that feeling for me that I kept this thing alive."

The "long-legged" Felix and a cast of characters familiar to a generation of TV viewers in the late 1950s and early 1960s.

EPILOGUE

OTTO MESSMER, who died at age ninety-one on October 28, 1983, did not pass away in obscurity. Indeed, his *New York Times* obituary the next day was more than double the length of Pat Sullivan's 1933 obit and featured a photo of Messmer with a Felix toy. The headline stating Messmer "Created 'Felix the Cat' " was carried by wire services and newspapers around the world.

Old-timers in the animation industry always knew of Otto Messmer's profound contributions to Felix the Cat and the art of character animation, but the general public's awareness of the cartoonist snowballed during the last years of his long life.

The first large-scale acknowledgment came in 1955 from the man who tried to hire Messmer away from Pat Sullivan twenty-seven years before: Walt Disney. For a program on animation history titled "The Story of the Animated Drawing," aired on the popular television show *Disneyland*, Disney finally got Messmer to work for him. He commissioned him to animate a cycle (consisting of twenty-eight drawings) of Felix walking.

Messmer's contract with Disney was cosigned by Pat Sullivan's nephew (as president of Felix the Cat Productions, Inc.), so the *Disneyland* script carefully described Felix as "Pat Sullivan's cartoon character." But as a photo of Sullivan cross-dissolved into Felix pacing back and forth, Walt Disney's voice-over commented: "This characteristic walk, animated by Sullivan's collaborator, Otto Messmer, became a laugh-provoking trademark." Over Felix's animation, a close-up of

Opposite: Otto Messmer in 1977. Collection of the author.

Messmer's face dissolved in and became part of a book titled *The Art of Animation.*

Disney's brief, charming tribute to the unsung artist who pioneered personality animation was the first time a large segment of the general populace had heard of Messmer, including a generation of future animators.

In 1967, the Montreal World's Fair (EXPO '67) hosted the Cinémathèque Québecoise Retrospective of Animation Cinema. Messmer was invited to attend as a special guest, and did so, along with five other elderly American animation pioneers, including John R. Bray, Walter Lantz, Dave Fleischer, Ub Iwerks, and Paul Terry. The retrospective hoped that its tribute to seventy-four-year-old Otto Messmer would "serve to establish in its true historical perspective the creative role he played along with Pat Sullivan during the making of [the Felix] films."

Nineteen seventy-six was a watershed year in publicity for Felix that connected Messmer with his art. *Variety*, in its seventieth anniversary issue (January 7, 1976), wrote about Messmer as one of the five most

Left to right: Dave Fleischer, Paul Terry, Walter Lantz, John R. Bray, and Otto Messmer at the EXPO '67 Animation Retrospective, Montreal 1967.

September 8, 1955

Dear Otto -

It has been a good many years since we last
met and needless to say, much has happened
during the interim.

This note is just to thank you for the cooperation you have given our boys who are working
on the TV subject, THE STORY OF THE
ANIMATED DRAWING. Your interest in help-
ing us with footage on this film is very much
appreciated and I hope you will be as pleased
with the finished results as we expect to be.

Sometime when I am in New York, I think it
would be wonderful if we could have a little
get together, so perhaps we can arrange something on one of these trips.

My regards and best wishes.

Sincerely

[signature]

Mr. Otto Messmer
Douglas Leigh Inc.
715 Fifth Avenue
New York 22, N. Y.

WD:DV

important "Pioneers of American Animation," and the September issue of the trade magazine *Millimeter* featured an extensive article on him. On September 24, Messmer appeared on the national television game show *To Tell the Truth* as the father of Felix the Cat.

Most significant that busy year were two major back-to-back retrospectives of Messmer's Felix the Cat films in the same month: April 13–18 at the Whitney Museum of American Art and April 25–27 at the Museum of Modern Art.

New York Times film critic Vincent Canby, reviewing the Whitney show on April 21, found Felix "one of the most dynamic personalities of the silent screen" and "a joyous rediscovery—"

> a truculent, resourceful man-cat with a walk that looks like the trudge of a bouncer in a waterfront saloon. As the Messmer backgrounds are simple to the point of being philosophic statements (one tree is all trees, one house is all houses, etc.), so too are the stories [which are] framing devices for the comic routines. . . . For reasons I don't quite understand, there is something immensely liberating about this sort of casual attitude toward narrative . . . in the comparatively primitive Messmer cartoons, the freedom of the form looks almost avant-garde.

Messmer appeared at the sold-out openings of both retrospectives, bowing silently to the crowd at the Whitney, and to an enthusiastic audience at MOMA, he reluctantly murmured the briefest of thank-yous. ("Like the cartoons, I am silent.")

After the MOMA and Whitney shows, Messmer was, in his words, "swamped" with media attention. He had been discovered and was treated like a living Rosetta stone, the vital missing link between pre- and post-Disney animation.

In 1977 I produced the documentary film *Otto Messmer and Felix the Cat*. The twenty-five-minute short, containing interviews with Messmer and Al Eugster intercut with clips from vintage Felix shorts, appeared on CBS *Camera Three* in November 1977 and on London's BBC 1 *Omnibus* in April the following year. It was screened at international film festivals and is part of the collections of numerous cinematheques and film libraries.

Otto Messmer demonstrates the famous Felix walk in 1976. Collection of the author.

Messmer was honored by his peers in October 1979 at the annual ASIFA (International Animation Film Society) ceremony in Hollywood. He was awarded its highest honor, the Winsor McCay trophy, "for long and distinguished service to the art of animation."

Subsequent tributes and film retrospectives in America, Canada, and Europe beckoned, but, as he headed toward his ninth decade, Messmer sent his regrets, blaming the frailties of old age. Each day's mail contained letters from fans around the world requesting an original drawing of the Cat; dutifully and happily, Otto Messmer spent his final years and days drawing Felix and (finally) autographing each and every one with his own name.

No celebrations marked the seventieth birthday of Felix the Cat in 1989. However, at Christmas, in F.A.O. Schwartz and other New York stores, whole walls of shelving filled with Felix dolls and merchandise smiled down on swirling holiday crowds. Felix had been off the big screen for over fifty years and the original films for which he gained fame are rarely seen outside of academic film study classes. Today, those who remember Felix as an animated character recall him from the TV series. Most young people have never seen Felix on a screen.

A brochure attached to the dolls contained the usual misinformation, claiming Felix was born in 1922, that Lindbergh carried Felix on his transatlantic flight, etc. The attempt to place Felix in a historical context wasn't necessary. The toys sell briskly because of the character's name (still as magical and potent as "Mickey Mouse") and his enduring appeal as a design.

Seventy years after Felix the Cat first appeared on the scene, Pat Sullivan, Otto Messmer, Harry Kopp, Burt Gillett, Charles Mintz, and Joe Oriolo—key players in his story—had passed away. But one remained.

In a quiet nursing home in upstate New York, ninety-five-year-old Margaret Winkler Mintz accepted with pleasure a Felix doll purchased by her daughter and son-in-law. Her memory clouded in benign senility, she did not recognize the character, nor did she recall Pat Sullivan, or even her husband, Charles Mintz. Only Otto Messmer's name brought a flicker of recognition. All the excitement, turmoil, and bitterness involved with Felix the Cat was gone, literally forgotten. Seated in a wheelchair, Mrs. Mintz held the soft pie-eyed toy, an image of something that was once so important to her and others, and absently caressed it.

Margaret Winkler Mintz in 1989, at age ninety-five. Collection of the author.

NOTES

For brevity, details of interviews conducted for this book are supplied only at the first citation; unless otherwise stated, subsequent quotations from the same source derive from the identical interview with that source

CHAPTER 1. HOLLYWOOD ON THE HUDSON

page 12 "Get into scene painting": Otto Messmer to JC, March 5, 1975.
        "Very gentle": Otto Messmer to JC, January 29, 1979.
        All quotations from Otto Messmer in this chapter are from interviews with the author on March 5, 1975, and January 29, 1979.
    15 "Ode": *Times,* unidentified periodical, c. 1914.

CHAPTER 2. DOWN UNDER

page 21 "Unsatisfactory": Probation Officer's Investigation. Supreme Court/Court of General Sessions. Indictments (May 1917, N–Z, shelf #106816), New York County Clerk's Office.
    22 "A damned hard struggle": *Melbourne Herald,* December 1925.
        "Sydney's oldest": *Daily Guardian* (Sydney), December 5, 1925.
    23 "The happiest": Dave Hechtlinger and Morris Kessler, *Commerce Caravel,* December 1930.
        "Were so unique": James S. Ryan to Supreme Court/Court of General Sessions, September 1, 1917.
    24 "As a matter of fact": *The Argus* (Melbourne), December 1, 1925.
        "In one of them": *Tit-Bits* (London), December 12, 1925.
        "A no-account": *Birmingham Mail,* May 21, 1924.
    25 "Pat sank": unidentified London clipping, c. 1925. Pat Sullivan scrapbook.
        "As fortune": *London Daily Standard* clipping, c. 1925. Pat Sullivan scrapbook.

CHAPTER 3. COMIC STRIP TO COMIC SCREEN, 1909–1916

page 27 "Several big": Mark Johnson to JC, August 20, 1989.

30 "Was a good salesman": Hal Walker to JC, July 24, 1989.

31 "Murdered by": *New York Times,* October 11, 1914.

33 "Though this": Klein, *Cartoonist Profiles,* March 1975.

34 "From a distance": André Martin, Ottawa 1976 Animation Festival program.

38 "So Chaplin": Otto Messmer to JC, sync sound transcript June 6, 1976, for documentary film *Otto Messmer and Felix the Cat* (1977).

CHAPTER 4. DERAILMENT, 1917–1919

page 42 "Brought one": Manhattan D.A. Closed Case File, Unit #115312, 1917.

44 "Speaking his mind": Arthur Markewich to JC, June 13, 1989.

"A man of": N.Y. Court of General Sessions transcript, September 13, 1917.

49 "That he was perhaps": Donald Crafton, *Before Mickey* (Cambridge, Mass.: MIT Press, 1982), p. 305.

CHAPTER 5. THE COMING OF THE CAT, 1919–1921

page 55 "The Jazz Age": Geoffrey Perrett, *America in the Twenties* (New York: Simon & Schuster, 1982), p. 147.

57 "Otto was": Hal Walker to Ralph Bowman, April 24, 1981.

"With its bowling alley": Peter Salwen, *Upper West Side Story* (New York: Abbeville Press, 1989), p. 204.

"Leader, not a boss": Hal Walker to JC, July 24, 1989.

58 "Was usually ossified": Hal Walker to Edwin Walker, circa 1978.

"Trying to escort": Hal Walker to JC, July 7, 1989.

"A weak man": Doris Messmer to JC, November 4, 1989.

60 "Margaret always": George Winkler to JC, December 3, 1989.

CHAPTER 6. THE WINKLER YEARS, 1921–1925

page 72 "Search for ways": Joe Adamson, *The Walter Lantz Story* (New York: G. P. Putnam's Sons, 1985), p. 38.

74 "Up-tempo": Geoffrey Perrett, *America in the Twenties,* p. 236.

83 "Pat Sullivan was": George Winkler to JC, December 3, 1989.

87 "Changed to the": *Los Angeles Examiner,* December 24, 1924.

90 "Is certainly": John Grant, *Encyclopedia of Walt Disney's Animated Characters.* (New York: Harper & Row, 1987), p. 15.

page 90 "Make their characters": Frank Thomas to JC, October 15, 1989.

   92 "Were dying": Erma Kopp Krents to JC, June 22, 1989.

   95 "Haven't you a": Bob Thomas, *Walt Disney—An American Original* (New York: Simon & Schuster, 1976), p. 78.

CHAPTER 7.   FELIX ON A HIGH ROLL, 1925–1928

page 100 "The accommodating": unidentified 1925 clipping in Pat Sullivan scrapbook: "Felix the Cat Has Many Things to Say."

   103 "Appearance is": Bela Balazs, *Theory of the Film* (New York: Dover Publications, 1970), p. 191.

   104 "Otto was": Al Eugster to JC, May 13, 1976.

   113 "It was quite": Otto Messmer to Mark Newgarden and John Mariano, May 7, 1980.

   114 "Messmer no longer": Donald Crafton, *Before Mickey*, p. 338.

   116 "You've got to": Ben Harrison to JC, January 25, 1978.

CHAPTER 8.   DOWN AND OUT, 1928–1933

page 121 "Before *The Jazz Singer*": Neal Gabler, *An Empire of Their Own* (New York: Crown Publishers, 1988), p. 145.

   123 "My gosh": Bob Thomas, *Walt Disney—An American Original*, p. 92.

   126 "The shapes": Ollie Johnston to JC, September 20, 1989.

   133 "Never jumped": Betty Jean Buckley to JC, September 14, 1989.

CHAPTER 9.   COMEBACK

page 139 "That guy's": Bob Thomas, *Walt Disney—An American Original*, p. 100.

   143 "What could": Leonard Maltin, *Of Mice and Magic* (New York: McGraw-Hill, 1980), p. 203.

   145 "An oversized": Robert Sellmer, *Life*, April 1, 1946.

   147 "Otto started": Will Friedwald, *Graffiti*, February 1985, p. 4.
       "Messmer did part": Joe Oriolo to JC, May 21, 1975.

EPILOGUE

page 156 "Serve to establish": press release no. 5, August 12, 1967. "Retrospective Mondiale du Cinéma d'animation."

   160 *Felix the Cat: The Movie,* a full-length cartoon written and produced by Don Oriolo (son of Joe Oriolo), featuring a computer-generated talking head

of Felix, premiered on January 26, 1989, at the Third Los Angeles International Animation Celebration; as of December 1989, the film was not in general distribution.

page 161 Margaret Winkler Mintz to JC, December 2, 1989. Mrs. Mintz died June 21, 1990.

SELECTED
BIBLIOGRAPHY

Adamson, Joe. *The Walter Lantz Story*. New York: G. P. Putnam's Sons, 1985.

Barrier, J. Michael. *Building a Better Mouse*. Washington, D.C.: Library of Congress, 1978.

Balazs, Bela. *Theory of the Film*. New York: Dover Publications, 1970.

Beck, Jerry, "Felix the Cat." *Animation Magazine*, Winter 1989.

Brion, Marcel. "Felix le chat ou la poésie créatrice." *Le Rouge et le Noir*. July 1928.

Bruen, Edward J. "Pat Sullivan's Cat—He Meows for All the World." *Cartoons and Movies Magazine*, vol. 31, no. 4, June 1927.

Canemaker, John. "Otto Messmer and Felix the Cat." *Millimeter*, September 1976, pp. 32ff.

———. *Otto Messmer and Felix the Cat*. (Film) 1977. Distributed by Phoenix Films and Video, New York City.

———. "Pioneers of American Animation." *Variety*, January 7, 1976.

———. *Winsor McCay—His Life and Art*. New York: Abbeville Press, 1987.

———. *The Animated Raggedy Ann and Andy*. Indianapolis: Bobbs-Merrill, 1977.

———. "Winsor McCay's Little Nemo and How a Mosquito Operates—Beginnings of Personality Animation." In *The Art of the Moving Image: An Anthology*, Charles Solomon, ed. Los Angeles: American Film Institute, 1987.

Carbaga, Leslie. *The Fleischer Story*. New York: Nostalgia Press, 1976.

Crafton, Donald. *Before Mickey: The Animated Film 1898–1928*. Cambridge, Mass.: MIT Press, 1982.

Culhane, Shamus. *Talking Animals and Other People*. New York: St. Martin's Press, 1986.

Falk, Nat. *How to Make Animated Cartoons*. New York: Foundation Books, 1941.

Friedwald, Will. "Joe Oriolo and Felix the Cat, or, Saturday Morning Animation Comes to New York." *Graffiti*, vol. 6, no. 1, February 1985.

Gabler, Neal. *An Empire of Their Own*. New York: Crown Publishers, 1988.

Grant, John. *Encyclopedia of Walt Disney's Animated Characters*. New York: Harper & Row, 1987.

Hay, Elizabeth. *Sambo Sahib*. Edinburgh: Paul Harris Publishing, 1981.

Hechtlinger, Dave, and Morris Kessler. "Boy! He's the Cat's—A Personal Interview with Pat Sullivan, Creator of Felix the Cat." *Commerce Caravel,* December 1930.

Klein, I. "Pioneer Animated Cartoon Producer Charles R. Bowers." *Cartoonist Profiles,* March 1975.

Lindesay, Vane. *The Inked-in Image.* Australia: Hutchinson, 1979.

Maltin, Leonard. *Of Mice and Magic: A History of American Animated Cartoons.* New York: McGraw-Hill, 1980.

Martin, André. "Barre l'introuvable." Ottawa International Animation Festival program, 1976.

Moritz, William. "Some Observations on Non-Objective and Non-Linear Animation." *Storytelling in Animation: The Art of the Animated Image,* vol. 2, John Canemaker, ed. Los Angeles: American Film Institute, 1988.

Musso, Barbara T. "Felix the Cat Bounces Back in New Career." *Pascack Valley Community Life* (N.J. newspaper), January 11, 1984.

Peary, Gerald, and Danny Peary, eds. *The American Animated Cartoon.* New York: E. P. Dutton, 1980.

Perrett, Geoffrey. *America in the Twenties.* New York: Simon & Schuster, 1982.

Salwen, Peter. *Upper West Side Story.* New York: Abbeville Press, 1989.

Schickel, Richard. *The Disney Version.* New York: Simon & Schuster, 1968.

Solomon, Charles. *Enchanted Drawings: The History of Animation.* New York: Alfred A. Knopf, 1989.

Thomas, Bob. *Walt Disney—An American Original.* New York: Simon & Schuster, 1976.

Thomas, Frank, and Ollie Johnston. *Disney Animation: The Illusion of Life.* New York: Abbeville Press, 1981.

SELECTED FILMOGRAPHY

This filmography is not definitive. Data are derived primarily from publicity releases and film booking guides, and there are a number of title/date gaps.

The date for *Feline Follies*, the first appearance of Master Tom (Felix the Cat's prototype), is based on a August 2, 1919, *Moving Picture World* article announcing the *Paramount Magazine* series and several animation producers hired to work on it, including Pat Sullivan. By March 1920, Master Tom was renamed "Felix" and Sullivan had a "long-term contract with Famous Players–Lasky Corporation to make cartoons for Paramount Magazine" (*MPW* 3/20/20). If the films appeared once a month starting in September 1919, it is possible that thirty or more were produced, depending on when Sullivan stopped in 1921, which is also not known. Except for *Feline Follies*, the *Paramount Magazine* films have never been researched.

Sullivan may also have independently produced one or two Felix "pilot" shorts in 1921, the same year he signed his first contract with distributor Margaret J. Winkler. An educated guess is that approximately 150 to 175 Felix films were made by Pat Sullivan and Otto Messmer between 1919 and 1930. Sullivan only began to copyright the films in 1925 with the Educational Film Series.

For the Felix film release dates from 1922 to 1928, I am grateful to Ron Magliozzi, Assistant Supervisor of the Film Study Center of the Museum of Modern Art in New York, who researched data in *Motion Picture News* Booking Guides in 1983.

1919–1921

Producer: Pat Sullivan
Distributor: Famous Players–Lasky (*Paramount Screen Magazine*)
Feline Follies September 1, 1919
Musical Mews 1919
(perhaps thirty or more Felix films during this period)

1922

Distributor: Margaret J. Winkler
Felix Saves the Day February 1, 1922 (perhaps a 1921 "pilot" film)
Felix at the Fair March 1, 1922
Felix Makes Good April 1, 1922
Felix All at Sea May 1, 1922
Felix in Love June 1, 1922
Felix in the Swim July 1, 1922
Felix Finds a Way August 1, 1922
Felix Gets Revenge September 1, 1922
Felix Wakes Up September 15, 1922
Felix Minds the Kid October 1, 1922
Felix Turns the Tide October 15, 1922
Felix on the Trail November 1, 1922
Felix Lends a Hand November 15, 1922
Felix Gets Left December 1, 1922
Felix in the Bone Age December 15, 1922

1923

Felix the Ghost Breaker January 1, 1923
Felix Wins Out January 15, 1923
Felix Tries for Treasure April 15, 1923
Felix Revolts May 1, 1923
Felix Calms His Conscience May 15, 1923
Felix the Globe Trotter June 1, 1923
Felix Gets Broadcasted June 15, 1923
Felix Strikes It Rich July 1, 1923
Felix in Hollywood July 15, 1923
Felix in Fairyland August 1, 1923
Felix Laughs Last August 15, 1923
Felix Fills a Shortage November 15, 1923
Felix the Goat Getter December 1, 1923
Felix Goes A-Hunting December 15, 1923

1924

Felix Loses Out January 15, 1924
Felix Hits the Hipps February 1, 1924
Felix Crosses the Crooks February 15, 1924
Felix Tries to Rest February 29, 1924

Felix Pinches the Pole May 1, 1924
Felix Puts It Over May 15, 1924
Felix Friend in Need June 1, 1924
Felix Baffled by Banjos June 15, 1924
Felix All Balled Up July 1, 1924
Felix Goes West August 1, 1924
Felix Finds Out November 1, 1924
Felix Brings Home the Bacon November 15, 1924
Felix Finishes First December 1, 1924
Felix Goes Hungry December 15, 1924
Felix Out of Luck (date unknown)
Felix Gets the Can (date unknown)
Felix Dopes It Out (date unknown)

1925

Felix Wins and Loses January 1, 1925
Felix All Puzzled January 15, 1925
Felix Follows the Swallows February 1, 1925
Felix Rests in Peace February 15, 1925

Distributor: Educational Films (release date and copyright date)
Felix the Cat Busts into Business September 6, 1925; © 11/03/25
Felix the Cat Trips Through Toyland September 20, 1925; © 11/19/25
Felix Trifles with Time August 23, 1925; © 10/13/25
Felix the Cat on the Farm October 4, 1925; © 11/18/25
Felix the Cat on the Job October 18, 1925; © 12/2/25
Felix the Cat in the Cold Rush November 1, 1925; © 12/29/25
Felix the Cat in Eats Are West November 15, 1925; © 12/29/25
Felix the Cat Tries the Trades November 29, 1925; © 1/14/26
Felix the Cat in at the Rainbow's End December 13, 1925; © 12/29/25
Felix the Cat Kept on Walking December 27, 1925; © 1/21/26

1926

Felix the Cat Spots the Spooks January 10, 1926; © 3/5/26
Felix the Cat Flirts with Fate January 24, 1926; © 3/2/26
Felix the Cat in Blunderland February 7, 1926; © 3/7/26
Felix Fans the Flames February 21, 1926; © 3/21/26
Felix the Cat Laughs It Off March 7, 1926; © 4/21/26
Felix the Cat Weathers the Weather March 21, 1926; © 4/21/26
Felix the Cat Uses His Head April 4, 1926; © 7/13/26

171

Felix the Cat Misses the Cue April 18, 1926; © 7/19/26
Felix the Cat Braves the Briny May 2, 1926; © 8/8/26
Felix the Cat in a Tale of Two Kitties May 16, 1926; © 12/9/26
Felix Scoots Through Scotland May 30, 1926; © 7/19/26
Felix the Cat Rings the Ringer June 13, 1926; © 7/26/26
Felix the Cat in School Daze June 27, 1926; © 8/9/26
Felix the Cat Seeks Solitude July 11, 1926; © 10/5/26
Felix the Cat Misses His Swiss July 25, 1926; © 9/15/26
Felix the Cat in Gym Gems August 8, 1926; © 10/5/26
Felix the Cat in Two Lips Time August 22, 1926; © 10/12/26
Felix the Cat in Scrambled Eggs September 5, 1926; © 10/11/26
Felix the Cat Shatters the Sheik September 19, 1926; © 11/19/26
Felix the Cat Hunts the Hunter October 3, 1926; © 11/8/26
Felix the Cat in Land O'Fancy October 17, 1926; © 11/19/26
Felix the Cat Busts a Bubble October 31, 1926; © 11/30/26
Felix the Cat in Reverse English November 14, 1926; © 12/13/26
Felix the Cat Trumps the Ace November 28, 1926; © 12/13/26
Felix the Cat Collars the Button December 12, 1926; © 12/24/26
Felix the Cat in Zoo Logic December 26, 1926; © 1/4/27

1927

Felix the Cat Dines and Pines January 9, 1927; © 1/11/27
Felix the Cat in Pedigreedy January 23, 1927; © 2/8/27
Felix the Cat in Icy Eyes February 6, 1927; © 2/16/27
Felix the Cat in Stars and Stripes February 1927; © 2/28/27
Felix the Cat Sees 'Em in Season March 6, 1927; © 3/8/27
Felix the Cat in Barn Yarns March 20, 1927; © 3/28/27
Felix the Cat in Germ Mania April 3, 1927; © 5/10/27
Felix the Cat in Sax Appeal April 27, 1927; © 7/27/27
Felix the Cat in Eye Jinks May 1, 1927; © 7/27/27
Felix the Cat as Romeeow May 15, 1927; © 5/16/27
Felix the Cat Ducks His Duty May 29, 1927; © 6/16/27
Felix the Cat in Dough-Nutty June 12, 1927; © 9/14/27
Felix the Cat in "Loco" Motive June 26, 1927; © 7/12/27
Felix the Cat in Art for Heart's Sake July 10, 1927; © 7/27/27
Felix the Cat in the Travel-Hog July 14, 1927; © 8/10/27
Felix the Cat, Jack of All Trades August 7, 1927; © 8/17/27
Felix the Cat, The Non-Stop Fright August 21, 1927; © 9/20/27
Felix the Cat in Wise Guise September 4, 1927; © 11/16/27
Felix the Cat in Flim Flam Films September 18, 1927; © 11/3/27
Felix the Cat Switches Witches October 2, 1927; © 11/7/27
Felix the Cat in No Fuelin' October 16, 1927; © 11/16/27

Felix the Cat in Daze and Knights October 30, 1927; © 11/28/27
Felix the Cat in Uncle Tom's Crabbin' November 13, 1927; © 11/28/27
Felix the Cat in Whys and Otherwhys November 27, 1927; © 12/27/27
Felix the Cat Hits the Deck December 11, 1927; © 12/19/27
Felix the Cat Behind in Front December 25, 1927; © 12/12/27

1928

Felix the Cat in the Smoke Scream January 8, 1928; © 1/8/28
Felix the Cat in Draggin' the Dragon January 22, 1928; © 2/26/28
Felix the Cat in the Oily Bird February 5, 1928; © 5/5/28
Felix the Cat in Ohm Sweet Ohm February 19, 1928; © 2/19/28
Felix the Cat in Japanicky March 4, 1928; © 3/14/28
Felix the Cat in Polly-tics March 18, 1928; © 3/18/28
Felix the Cat in Comicalamities April 1, 1928; © 5/7/28
Felix the Cat in Sure-Locked Homes April 15, 1928; © 4/15/28
Felix the Cat in Eskimotive April 19, 1928; © 6/4/28
Felix the Cat in Arabiantics May 13, 1928; © 5/13/28
Felix the Cat in In and Out-Laws May 27, 1928; © 7/27/28
Felix the Cat in Outdoor Indore June 10, 1928; © 7/21/28
Felix the Cat in Futuritzy June 24, 1928; © 7/24/28
Felix the Cat in Astronomeows July 8, 1928; © 9/17/28
Felix the Cat in Jungle Bungles July 22, 1928; © 9/18/29
Felix the Cat in the Last Life August 5, 1928; © 9/18/28

Distributor: Copley Pictures Corporation
A number of previously released films reissued with sound tracks, plus:
Felix the Cat in False Vases c. 1930
Felix the Cat Woos Whoopee c. 1930 (or 1928)
Felix the Cat in April Maze c. 1930
Felix the Cat in Oceantics c. 1930 (or 1925)
Felix the Cat in Skulls and Sculls c. 1930
Felix the Cat in Forty Winks c. 1930
Felix the Cat in Tee-Time c. 1930
Hootchy Kootchy Parlais Vous c. 1930

Producer: Van Beuren Corporation (Rainbow Parade series)
Distributor: RKO
Felix the Cat and the Goose That Laid the Golden Eggs February 7, 1936
Neptune Nonsense March 20, 1936
Bold King Cole May 29, 1936

173

Producer: Joe Oriolo, Felix the Cat Productions, Inc.
Distributor: Trans-Lux Television Productions, Inc.
Series of 260 three-minute *Felix the Cat* cartoons produced for television, 1959–1960.

Producer: John Canemaker
Distributor: Phoenix Films and Video, Inc.
Otto Messmer and Felix the Cat, 1977 documentary film featuring on-camera interviews with Otto Messmer and Al Eugster, and clips from 1920s *Felix* films.

Producer: Don Oriolo, Felix the Cat Productions, Inc.
Felix the Cat: The Movie, feature-length animated film produced in 1989.

INDEX

ABOUT THE AUTHOR

John Canemaker is an animator, filmmaker, teacher, author, and lecturer. His animation appears in the Academy Award–winning HBO documentary *You Don't Have to Die*, Warner's *The World According to Garp*, Yoko Ono's *John Lennon Sketchbook*, and the forthcoming IBM-sponsored television series *The Creative Spirit*. In 1984, the Museum of Modern Art honored his film work with a "Cineprobe" retrospective.

A leading authority on the history and aesthetics of animation, Canemaker has written four books and over a hundred articles for leading periodicals. He has also written and hosted programs for CBS and The Disney Channel.

Canemaker has been a visiting lecturer at Yale University and currently is head of the animation program at New York University's Tisch School of the Arts. NYU's Bobst Library is home to the John Canemaker Animation Collection, a unique resource for animation scholars and students, containing oral-history audio tapes, interview transcripts, clippings, production data, books, and original art donated by Canemaker from nearly two decades' worth of his personal research materials.